LOST TREASURES *of* INDIANA

By Joseph S. Pete

Reedy Press
PO Box 5131
St. Louis, MO 63139, USA
reedypress.com

Library of Congress Control Number: 2025936319

ISBN: 9781681066066

Images courtesy of author or believed to be in the public domain unless otherwise noted.

Front cover photos: *Top left* courtesy Ball State University Archives, *top middle* courtesy Ball State University, *second row right* courtesy LaPorte County Historian, *third row righ*t Elkhart County Historical Society, *bottom left* courtesy Michigan City Historical Society, bottom right courtesy Wikimedia Commons

Printed in Canada

25 26 27 28 29   5 4 3 2 1

DEDICATION

This book is dedicated to my late brother, Tom, who was a true cinephile, a brilliant comedian who cracked everyone up, and a bright light that shall never burn out.

TABLE OF CONTENTS

Acknowledgments vi

Introduction 1

Food and Drink 2

- Restaurants 4
- Theme Restaurants 36
- Bars and Breweries 39
- Steak Houses 44
- Diners and Drive-Ins 47
- Fast Food 51
- Local Products 54

Entertainment 58

- Amusement Parks 60
- Sports Venues 64
- Sports Teams 68
- Film 73
- Music 80
- Live Entertainment 86
- Museums 94
- Art 98

Circle Square
Courtesy of Wikimedia Commons

Retail **102**
Retail Stores 104
Department Stores 109
Malls 114
Hotels 117

Media **122**
Television 124
Print 128

Community **136**
Natural Wonders 138
Railroads 144
Carmakers 147
Industrial 151
Hospitals and Health Care 158
Schools and Churches 162
Forts 168
Notable Places 171

Index **182**

ACKNOWLEDGMENTS

The great philosopher Snoop Dogg once proclaimed, "Last but not least, I wanna thank me/ I wanna thank me for believing in me/ I wanna thank me for doing all this hard work/ I wanna thank me for having no days off/ I wanna thank me for, for never quitting." That's funny, and there's a smidge of truth to it, but the reality is any endeavor as large or as ambitious as a book takes a proverbial village. I extend my heartfelt thanks to everyone who agreed to be interviewed, made suggestions, offered insights, or supplied photos for this book that Reedy Press asked me to write. In particular, I would like to thank the Indiana Historical Society; PoCo Muse; the Westchester Township History Museum; the La Porte County Historical Society Museum; the Indianapolis-Marion County Public Library; the Evansville Vanderburgh Public Library; the Elkhart County Historical Museum; the Gary Public Library; Historic Indianapolis; the Merrillville-Ross Township Historical Society; the Michigan City Historical Society; the Hammond Public Library; the Lowell Public Library; the Allen County Public Library; Purdue University Libraries; Indiana University Libraries; the Eckhart Public Library; the St. Joseph County Public Library; the Westchester Township History Museum; the Marion Public Library; the Monon-Railroad Historical-Technical Society; the Monroe County Public Library; the Monroe County History Center; the Morgan County History Center and Museum; the Floyd County Historical Society; fellow authors like Jane Ammeson, Ken Schoon, and Carrie Steinweg; and everyone who helped. Sorry to anyone who may have been omitted due to space constraints; I still very much appreciate you. I would like to thank my wife, Meredith, for copyediting my manuscript and my daughter, Harper, for her support, such as by declaring "Dada book" every time she sees one of my books. I would like to thank everyone who's ever read and supported my work, whether my books or my writing for *The Times of Northwest Indiana.* And I would like to thank all the hardworking people in the state of Indiana, a place where people quietly go about their jobs and get things done. If nothing else, I hope I've made a small contribution to recording the Hoosier State's rich history.

INTRODUCTION

A television commercial jingle that once played incessantly proclaimed there's more than corn in Indiana. The Hoosier State has long been dogged by nagging perceptions that it's nothing more than an endless flat expanse of cornfields that fade into the horizon. That's not the full story, since any good farmer knows you have to rotate soybeans through to preserve the health of the soil. And Indiana's topography is actually far more varied, ranging from the sand dunes that flank Lake Michigan to the wooded hills of Southern Indiana. Though often perceived as landlocked, the Hoosier State has ports along the Great Lake and the Ohio River that rank among the busiest in the country. Indiana is often thought of as a Midwestern agricultural state on the "I-Belt" with Iowa and neighboring Illinois, but it does more than feed the rest of the country. Industry has long been the largest source of employment in the Hoosier State. Indiana makes more steel than any other state; nearly every RV in the country; and also cars, pharmaceuticals, gummi bears, and countless other products. It's given the world many inventions, including Wonder Bread, the Gatling Gun, Prozac, seat belts, sliced bacon, washing machines, and push-button car radios. It made major early contributions to fields like aviation, ecology, and horseless carriages. It's been a cradle of vice presidents, astronauts, and cartoon cats who hate Mondays but not lasagna. It's produced or been home to greats in many fields, including Kurt Vonnegut Jr., Larry Bird, Madam C. J. Walker, Jane Pauley, John Wooden, Adam Driver, Alvah Curtis Roebuck, Michael Graves, Robert Indiana, John Green, Jenna Fischer, Jim Gaffigan, Will Shortz, and Birch Bayh, who got more constitutional amendments passed than anyone who was not a Founding Father. The Hoosier State helped launch the illustrious careers of Hank Aaron, Wayne Gretzky, and Wolfgang Puck. A basketball-crazed state home to the world's largest high school gymnasium in New Castle and 10 of the country's 12 largest high school gyms, it's inspired classic sports films like *Hoosiers* and *Rudy*. Indiana is why Wrigley Field has ivy, why Harley-Davidson motorcycles are called hogs, and why tires are made of rubber. It's why we have gas pumps, rearview mirrors, and tomato juice, which a chef invented at the French Lick Springs Hotel in 1917 and which the Kemp Company in Kokomo first canned as baby food a decade later. As Kurt Vonnegut observed in *Cat's Cradle*, "I don't know what it is about Hoosiers. But wherever you go there is always a Hoosier doing something very important there."

{FOOD and DRINK}

Indiana is known for homegrown, homestyle cuisine like the pork tenderloin sandwich, persimmon pie, and sugar cream pie. It has produced many nationally popular foods, like Orville Redenbacher's Original Gourmet Popping Corn, Red Gold Ketchup, Hurst's HamBeens, Wonder Bread, Jet-Puffed Marshmallows, and the "leviathan of legumes" Van Camp's Pork and Beans, as *Indianapolis Monthly* put it, as well as restaurant chains like Papa John's, Steak 'n Shake, and technically Kentucky Fried Chicken, since Col. Harland Sanders is actually an Indiana native. It has been home to many iconic eateries, like the Slippery Noodle Inn in Indianapolis, Payne's in Gas City, Wagner's Village Inn in Oldenburg, Beef House in Covington, Ivanhoe's in Upland, Triple XXX in West Lafayette, Coney Island in Fort Wayne, and St. Elmo Steak House in Indianapolis, whose fiery shrimp cocktail is the stuff of legends. *Indianapolis Monthly* once quipped that the secret ingredients were horseradish, ketchup, and sadism. Indianapolis alone had many classic drive-ins where people made memories, like Blue Ribbon, Jack 'n Jill's, and Al Green's, where diners joked that they screened movies for free because the service was so slow. Many eateries gained legendary status before the competition intensified in the late 20th century, simply because there were fewer places to go out to eat. Many landmark eateries did not stand the test of time but remain fondly remembered.

Courtesy of Wikimedia Commons

Scotty's Brewhouse
Courtesy of Shawna Pierson

Courtesy of
Wikimedia Commons

Mudbugs
Courtesy of Road Tips

Celebration Station
Courtesy of Merrillville Historical Society

RESTAURANTS

Diners in Indiana can savor a meal everywhere from high-end steak houses with white tablecloths and wine cellars to the Gnaw Mart in Gnaw Bone, a gas station famed for its pork tenderloins. The Hoosier State is home to every type of dining experience and cuisine. From the fried chicken in Northern Indiana's Amish Country to the rolled oysters at KingFish overlooking the Ohio River, there's something for every palate. There's German food in Jasper, Tibetan fare in Bloomington, Cerulean's acclaimed bento boxes in Winona Lake, and even Evansville's fried brain sandwiches. However, some of the state's most beloved restaurants live on only in memory, like Hammond's Phil Smidt's, which was long famed for its lake perch and frog legs that came out of nearby Lake Michigan.

Mandarin Inn

The Mandarin Inn was a Chinese restaurant that also was well-known for its steaks in the Art Deco Ma-Co Building on College Avenue in Indianapolis. Opening in the 1940s, the Mandarin Inn was managed by Daniel M. Lee, who later opened the Lotus Garden down the street in the Town & Country Shopping Center at Allisonville Road and North Keystone. The Mandarin Inn claimed to be Indiana's oldest Chinese restaurant. By 1960, the *Indianapolis Times* described it as one of the city's oldest restaurants. It offered carryout specials of chow mein and chop suey by the quart. The menu also included Cantonese, Szechuan, egg foo yong, and sweet-and-sour dishes. It had a spacious dining room, banquet rooms for private parties, and a bar with exotic South Seas cocktails. It closed in the late 1980s, and the building came down a few years later.

Courtesy of Ball State University Library

Frank-N-Stein

Frank-N-Stein in Gary's Miller Beach neighborhood attained a masterful degree of wordplay. The roadside eatery just off the highway at US 12 and US 20 featured Frankenstein's monster holding a frank and a frosty stein of foamy root beer. The 20-foot-tall visual pun was right across the street from a competing A&W with basically the same menu. The hot dog and root beer joint ran afoul of Universal Studios, which made the Frankenstein and other classic horror film franchises. It sent a cease-and-desist letter. Frank-N-Stein settled the case by cutting off the neck bolts and changing a scar on the forehead, which were unique to Universal's cinematic version of the Mary Shelley classic. It was a popular dining spot in the 1960s and 1970s, and the Frankenstein statue remained long after it closed, but the local landmark was removed at some point in the 1990s.

Courtesy of Dave Distler

Courtesy of Wikimedia Commons

Rodini Restaurant and Cocktail Lounge

Celebrities like Dennis Farina, Sam Elliott, Mike Ditka, Steve McMichael, the entire Dallas Cowboys football team, and Bishop Dale Melczek of the Catholic Diocese of Gary dined at Rodini's in Michigan City. Indiana governors like Evan Bayh and Mitch Daniels stopped there, as did presidential candidate John Edwards and many college football coaches coming to play against University of Notre Dame in nearby South Bend. The Greek immigrant Larry Fegaras, who came to America when he was 13 years old and started peeling potatoes for the chance to borrow a bicycle, started the restaurant at 4125 Franklin Street. He also launched the Galveston Steakhouse near the Lake Michigan lakefront. The dimly lit Rodini featured dark woods, red carpeting, and a varied menu that blended a high-end steak house with Greek diner fare. It served veal Parmesan but also chicken livers, as well as the popular flaming saganaki appetizer. Fegaras decided in 2015 to shutter Rodini's after 44 years because of the proliferation of chain restaurants and his advancing age but said he had loved every minute of it.

Strongbow Inn

Strongbow Inn was a landmark roadhouse on US 30 in Valparaiso where it was Thanksgiving every day. The restaurant was known for its turkey dinners, which were as fresh and local as it gets. The turkeys were raised at a farm right across the street. A landmark that was featured on postcards, the restaurant at 2405 US 30 lasted for 75 years but eventually was turned into the Market wedding venue and comedy club and later was purchased by Valparaiso University and torn down. Opened by Dr. Walter and Bess Thrun, it was named after a Potawatomi chief who had lived there in the 1800s. It served traditional carved turkey, turkey schnitzel, and turkey potpie along with sides like cranberry sauce, stuffing, and freshly baked dinner rolls. It went through an estimated 250,000 pounds of turkey a year.

Courtesy of PoCo Muse

La Tour

Courtesy of the Indiana State Library

Wolfgang Puck landed a gig early in his career at La Tour in Indianapolis. The French restaurant atop the Indiana National Bank Building was a destination for special occasions for nearly two decades. It was one of a few skyscraper restaurants at the time, including the Eagle's Nest atop the Hyatt Regency and the Carousel in the Hilton overlooking Monument Circle. La Tour sat on the 35th floor of the 37-story marble-and-glass tower, sharing the space with the Teller's Cage Lounge. More than 140 diners could eat in the dining room with panoramic views. In the 1970s, the haute cuisine was prepared by Puck, an Austrian who would become one of the first celebrity chefs. He left Indianapolis after a year for Los Angeles, where he popularized gourmet pizza at Spago. The formal La Tour was replaced by the more casual Pennsylvania Street Bar and Grill in 1992.

Bear's Place

Courtesy of the *Indiana Daily Student*

Bear's Place Ale House & Eatery closed in 2022 after a half century serving Indiana University students. The watering hole and restaurant was located right off campus. It was an iconic spot on 3rd Street by the Village Pantry, Soma, and the Indiana Shop bookstore. Opened in 1972, Bear's Place was especially known for its burgers, wings, wide selection of craft beer, and the "almost world-famous" Hairy Bears, sweetened 32-ounce drinks that could be loaded up with as many shots as one dared to down. It often hosted comedy, Ryder Film Series movie screenings, and live music, long serving as a jazz club where jazz professors from the School of Music down the street took the stage for the popular Jazz Fables series. It later hosted indie and alternative rock bands and other musical genres. The IU Foundation bought it a year after it closed.

Courtesy of Pixabay

Chaparral Cafe

The Chaparral Cafe was long a staple in Shelbyville that closed in 2025 after 58 years when the owner decided to hang it up. Specializing in home-cooked, country-style fare, the traditional diner served bacon and eggs, biscuits and gravy, fried chicken, and pork tenderloin sandwiches. Owner Shirley Bailey arrived at 3:30 a.m. each morning to start cooking breakfast. She created the famous Stardust Breaded Tenderloin, a spin on one of Indiana's signature dishes, while working at the Stardust Drive-In Theatre. The hand-pounded and -breaded pork tenderloin patty was touted as "bigger than your head" and earned the Chaparral Cafe a place on the Indiana Foodways Alliance's Tenderloin Trail, drawing tenderloin enthusiasts from across the state. The restaurant was named after the western show *The High Chaparral* that was popular in the 1960s.

King Cole

The King Cole was a destination for fancy dining for nearly 70 years in downtown Indianapolis. The place for a swanky night out occupied the basement of the 10-story Art Deco Kahn Building, which was designed by Vonnegut, Bohn, and Mueller. The Seville restaurant opened there in 1929. In the 1950s, it was rebranded as the King Cole after being remodeled into a more formal space with a strict dress code. It served steaks, seafood, racks of lamb, and French continental cuisine. Waiters flambéed crepes suzette and cherries jubilee at the table. The restaurant hosted notable guests like Ted Koppel and Vincent Price, bringing a phone to the table if they had to take an important call. An outbreak of Legionnaires' disease in 1979 tanked its reputation, and changing tastes made it less popular before it closed in 1994. It was replaced by the popular Nicky Blaine's Cocktail Lounge.

Courtesy of Indiana Landmarks

Benjamin's

Benjamin's Coffeehouse and Bakeshop, named after Benjamin Franklin, was a staple on the courthouse square in downtown Franklin for more than three decades. The coffee shop on East Court Street served a range of espresso drinks, teas, bubble teas, flavored sodas, and Hershey's hand-dipped ice cream. It had a selection of paninis and deli sandwiches like the Flying Kite chicken salad croissant for the lunch crowd. A quaint establishment in a quaint downtown, it had alfresco seating, pastries behind a glass counter, and a walk-up counter. It also sold shirts, jewelry, and artisan goods. Local art lined the walls in the narrow shotgun-style space. Students from Franklin College, attorneys headed to court, and townies all mingled in the cozy, welcoming coffee shop. Under new ownership, Benjamin's closed in 2024 after more than 30 years due to increased competition in the coffee space, a slow winter, and a big bet on an influx of eclipse tourists that did not pan out.

Atz Ice Cream

Atz Ice Cream started in Kendallville in 1922 and became a Northeast Indiana staple. The Atz family produced ice cream for nearly a century at the Puritan Ice Cream plant in Kendallville, shipping it within a 100-mile radius until the refrigeration system stopped working in 2011. The family opened the first Atz's Ice Cream Shoppe in Fort Wayne in 1956, running two ice cream parlors at Anthony Boulevard and Tillman Road that served more than 50 types of ice cream and sherbet. Popular flavors included happy tracks, tin roof, and banana pudding. PBS Food ranked Atz Ice Cream as one of Indiana's best ice cream places shortly before it shuttered both Fort Wayne locations in 2014. Longtime owner Norman Atz died a few years later.

Courtesy of Wikimedia Commons

Bronko's
Restaurant & Lounge

The significant other of a waitress at Bronko's in Crown Point always popped a quarter in the jukebox to play "Sea of Love" to let her know when he arrived. Hillary Clinton famously did a boilermaker—a shot of whiskey with a beer chaser—at Bronko's during the 2008 Democratic primary, eventually narrowly beating out Barack Obama, who would carry the Hoosier State in the general election. The longtime restaurant brimmed with stories. An institution that started in Gary in the 1960s, Bronko's was known especially for its pizza and fried chicken, but it also had ribs, fish, and sandwiches. It packed them in for 55 years before closing in 2015. A few spots have popped up to sell Bronko's Pizza in Hebron and Schererville, but the pizza recipe is really all that's left of the longtime community gathering place.

Courtesy of Wikimedia Commons

Jong Mea

Jong Mea Chinatown Restaurant claimed to offer authentic Chinese fare that the other Chinese restaurants that subsequently sprang up in Indianapolis imitated. Its sign was a North Meridian Street landmark that claimed it was nationally famous. Run by the Chin family for decades, the Chinese restaurant served Cantonese food for dining in or carryout. It had tropical cocktails, private banquet rooms, and a white-tablecloth dining experience. Irving Chin founded the family-run restaurant that also had locations in Columbus, Ohio, and Mansfield, Ohio. The house specialties included the Jong Mea Har that blended fantail shrimp and bacon and the Jong Mea Chow that mixed baby shrimp, Chinese vegetables, and snow peas into fried rice. In addition to chow mein and chop suey, it served American fare like lake trout, fried chicken, veal, liver, roast pork, and turkey. It closed in 1998.

Courtesy of Freepik

Q.L.'S BAR-B-QUE

Q.L.'s Bar-B-Que cooked some of the best barbecue in Muncie for more than 40 years. Q. L. and Willa Mae Stevens operated the East Central Indiana landmark from the 1970s to the early 2010s out of their white cinderblock structure that Q. L. built himself by his home on Wolfe Street, just down the hill from the White River. It was known for ribs, chicken, turkey, and other slow-cooked meats. Q. L. Stevens was a Kentucky native who started barbecuing "whole steers and hogs" at the age of 6, learning the art of barbecue from family and friends. He tried his hand at mining and professional boxing before moving to Indiana and eventually landing a job at the Chevy plant in Muncie. He launched the business after having three kids, needing a side income to pay the bills.

Merrill's Hi-Decker

The DJ Dick Sumner broadcast his radio show on Indianapolis's number one teen station in the 1950s from a glass booth on the roof of Merrill's Hi-Decker across from the Indiana State Fairgrounds. It reportedly inspired Wolfman Jack's booth in *American Graffiti.* The restaurant at 38th and Fall Creek sold burgers and milkshakes in a building shaped like a stack of records. A neon "WIBC 1070 On Your Dial" marquee beckoned passing motorists. The pompadoured Sumner played the latest rock-and-roll hits and hosted a nightly "Make It or Break It" segment in which diners would honk to vote whether a vinyl record should continue to be played on future shows or broken. He interviewed local bands that played in the parking lot, allowing restaurant patrons to come over and ask their own questions. He read short stories at midnight, often by Edgar Allan Poe.

Courtesy of the Indiana Historical Society

The Patio

Courtesy of Freepik

The Patio in Merrillville served steak, seafood, and strong cocktails for more than 40 years. The restaurant at 7706 Broadway was once a place where politicians like US Senator Evan Bayh and House Majority Leader Representative Dick Gephardt hobnobbed. Customers frequented the Merrillville landmark for banquets, weddings, and showers. It originally opened as Church's Restaurant and hosted live bands and dancing, serving as a nightlife hot spot until switching its focus to fine dining and catering. Owner Debra Batistatos said the customer base aged and no longer stayed out as late or drank as much, sealing the restaurant's fate. It grilled its last steak in 2015.

Courtesy of Freepik

Grandy's

Grandy's was a homey chain of diners that served breakfast fare with a Southern flair in Jasper, Oakland City, Evansville, and the wider Tri-State area. It was especially known for country fried steak, biscuits, pancakes, and Sinnamon Rolls. Dinner fare included pot roast, fried chicken, mashed potatoes with gravy, buttery corn, fresh-baked rolls, and other comfort food. It opened in 1972 and aimed to serve food like Grandma used to make for Sunday supper. The last two Tri-State Grandy's on First Avenue in Evansville and across the Ohio River in Henderson, Kentucky, closed in 2025. A manager told the online publication Fingers, Fork, Knife & Spoon Evansville that the business never recovered after the pandemic.

Jazz at the Station

Jazz at the Station was a novel restaurant and jazz club at 11th Street and North Walnut in Bloomington. It hosted live jazz acts in an old train station on the tracks. Catering to a more sophisticated adult audience than the local college crowd, it promised evenings of dinner, drinks, and dancing. Located in the former Illinois Central Railroad Freight Depot along an elevated railroad, it offered fine dining and hosted many jazz acts, including faculty members from the acclaimed Indiana University School of Music. The venue proved to be short-lived, but Bloomington still has a lively jazz scene.

Courtesy of Freepik

MACRI'S ITALIAN VILLAGE

Macri's Italian Village served traditional Italian fare in a romantic candlelit setting with checkerboard tablecloths. The authentic Italian eatery opened in a former house at 2343 North Meridian Street in Indianapolis in 1951. It lasted more than 40 years, later moving to a shopping center at Keystone and 52nd Street and then to the Carmel Motel on US 31 and Old Meridian Street. It offered an expansive antipasti buffet and deep-fried carrots, hosted guests like Robert F. Kennedy, and was known for its colorful owner, the World War II veteran Silvo "John" Macri. He toured around the country as a numerologist and advised celebrities like Liberace and Rita Moreno. He owned the restaurant for nearly its entire run. It closed in 1996 shortly after he died.

Courtesy of Wikimedia Commons

Shakey's Pizza Parlor

Shakey's Pizza Parlor was a beloved pizzeria with locations in Highland, Merrillville, and Valparaiso that evokes intense nostalgia whenever it gets brought up. The California-based chain originally opened as "Ye Public House." It served pizza and beer in an old-timey environment in which employees dressed like singers in a barbershop quartet and ragtime and jazz played in the background. The family-oriented Shakey's had arcade games for kids, picnic tables families could gather around, and a popular Sunday pizza buffet, capturing much of the after-church crowd as well as many youth sports teams. Customers could watch the pizza being made through windows. A sign in the kitchen jokingly warned the chefs were lip-readers so diners should watch what they said. The entertainment also included a piano player in a straw hat and vintage movies, including Laurel and Hardy comedies. The chain still has a smattering of locations left today, but none remain in Indiana, where it's one of the most fondly remembered pizza places on social media.

Cafe Pizzaria

The cozy and spelling-challenged Cafe Pizzaria baked pizza and stromboli on Kirkwood Avenue in Bloomington starting in 1953, becoming a local favorite that was a short walk from the Sample Gates on the Indiana University campus. The dine-in pizza place on Bloomington's main strip was a Bloomington tradition that fed hungry IU students for more than 70 years. It closed in 2024 just after winning the Bloomington *Herald-Times* award for best pizza in the college town full of iconic pizza joints, beating out Bucceto's Pizza Pasta and Mother Bear's Pizza. It was hailed as a Bloomington icon and a face on the Mount Rushmore of the Bloomington food scene with one longtime customer saying it was the first number he memorized after his home number. The owners decided to retire to spend more time with family.

Courtesy of Wikimedia Commons

Key West Shrimp House

Key West Shrimp House was a go-to place where Hoosiers headed for seafood in Indianapolis, Anderson, Bloomington, Madison, and Gas City. The flagship Key West Shrimp House was located in a barnacle-encrusted steamship on South Madison Avenue by Manual High School on Indianapolis's South Side. The seafood restaurant flew a cross-and-bones pirate flag outside and offered shrimp, lobster, Seafood Norfolk, hush puppies, and stuffed twice-baked potatoes in a nautically themed building that opened in 1950. Every meal came with lobster bisque, garlic bread, and dill pickles, as well as apricot bars for dessert. It moved to the redeveloped Union Station in downtown Indy in 1986. Its ads, featuring dancing shrimps, claimed it offered "pedigreed seafood and aristocratic steaks famous from coast to coast."

macdon512 via Flickr

Gray Brothers Cafeteria

The old-school Gray Brothers Cafeteria in Mooresville cooked up "homestyle meals with a hometown feel" since 1944. The cafeteria served hearty fare like fried chicken, homemade noodles, Roast Beef Manhattans, and roast pork tenderloins with sides like mashed potatoes and gravy, green beans, and buttered sweet corn. It served a wide variety of pies for dessert, including rhubarb, lemon meringue, blackberry, and butterscotch cream. After 80 years, the owners decided in 2024 to close the flagship eatery in Mooresville and looked at opening grab-and-go locations elsewhere after finding success with a Gray Brothers Cafeteria Baked Goods to Go location in Avon. The 17,787-square-foot restaurant on Indiana Avenue was listed for $10 million.

Ducky's Family Restaurant

Restaurant Impossible's Robert Irvine tried to save Ducky's Family Restaurant in Kokomo, but to no avail. The family-owned restaurant had a run of more than 30 years and was passed down from father to son. But it started to struggle, requiring intervention. Irvine made a number of changes like getting rid of canned and frozen food when it appeared in season 7 of the long-running reality series. Ducky's was able to boost sales and hire more staff, but the gains proved short-lived. The restaurant shuttered in 2013 after falling behind on taxes and going too deep into debt.

Bill's Bar-B-Que

Bill's Bar-B-Que cooked its meats low and slow. The barbecue joint in Elkhart started as a food truck in 1982, moved the trailer to Waterfall Drive, and then moved to the parking lot of Henry's Corner Store. It became a brick-and-mortar joint in a little red shack on Franklin Street, then relocated to Roseland, then to Cassopolis Street, and finally to Benham Avenue. The family-owned restaurant smoked many different meats, including brisket, rib tips, pulled pork, and chicken. Founder Alfred Lee named it after his son, William, who started cooking his own burgers and fries when he was in the fourth grade and eventually inherited the business. It was highlighted in WNDU's popular *Michiana Eats* feature. Some even claimed the brisket was better than what's available in Texas. It closed after more than 40 years in 2025.

Hawthorn Restaurant

The Hawthorn Restaurant was a popular dining spot for the media and ad industries in Indianapolis, as it was nestled between the television stations along North Meridian Street at a time when it was flanked by restaurants and eateries. The restaurant had modest prices and five separate dining rooms, each with its own unique theme. Richard Adams owned the restaurant and decorated it with photos of hawthorn trees from his backyard. It also had a faux tree in the bar with a bough of dollar bills hanging from the ceiling. It was popular, especially for lunch. The menu included steaks, glazed ham loaf, butterscotch rolls, sour cream raisin pie, and fruit salad with poppy-seed dressing.

Courtesy of Boston Public Library

CHEZ JEAN

Chez Jean Restaurant and Inn in Camby prepared classic French cuisine for a half century in an incongruous spot at a roadside motel off State Road 67 in a largely rural area on Marion County's southwest side. The Mobil four-star establishment opened in 1957. After cutting his teeth on American restaurants in Louisville, French native Jean Milesi opened the fine-dining restaurant and 12-room motel 20 miles from downtown Indy near the Indianapolis International Airport. One customer noted the rooms were cheap and the meals expensive but excellent. Milesi retired in 1997. American Culinary Foundation Chef of the Year Carl Huckaby took over, expanding the menu and opening a second location on Indy's South Side. Chez Jean closed in 2009, when it was the last traditional full-service French restaurant left in the area. The Plainfield Fire Department later burned down the building for a training exercise.

Courtesy of Mooresville Public Library

Sir Beef

Sir Beef claimed to serve "one of the world's finest roast beef sandwiches." Founded in 1967, it had a few Indiana locations, including Evansville, Anderson, and Lafayette. Farmer's Daughters Enterprises in Evansville tried to take the restaurant chain national during a time when roast beef sandwiches were hugely popular, but it did not pan out. Similar to Rax Roast Beef, Sir Beef had a Sir Beef sandwich, kosher corned beef sandwiches on rye, a Sir Ham with Oxford baked ham, pickled beets, and cheesecake. It bought the meat from a butcher every day, started slow-cooking it at 6 a.m., and sliced it thin. Sir Beef locations started closing in the 1980s and 1990s. Casey's Dugout in Evansville now displays one of the old Sir Beef signs. Nostalgic fans say that Lion's Choice around St. Louis tastes pretty much the same.

Knobby's Restaurant

Knobby's Restaurant provided more than 50 years of memories. The drive-in restaurant on Indianapolis's Keystone Avenue was founded by a World War II veteran in 1951 and grilled burgers and pork tenderloin sandwiches. It opened a second location on North Shadeland Avenue on the east side that rebranded as Knobby's Mai Tai restaurant to take advantage of the tiki trend and served famous visitors like Johnny Cash and Colonel Sanders. It had grass-thatched walls meant to evoke a South Seas paradise, a tropical saltwater fish tank, and sarong-wrapped waitresses. Ukulele players and Polynesian dancers performed on weekends. It served Hawaiian and Cantonese cuisine prepared by chef Tomie Moi, who the restaurant stole away from Chicago's famous Edgewater Beach Hotel. The menu included Polynesian duck and exotic cocktails like Rattlesnake Revenge, Satan's Sin, and Knobby's Eruption, a rum-based drink served in a bowl that was lit aflame. The last Knobby's location closed in 2001 and was replaced with a BP gas station.

Courtesy of Indiana Landmarks

Laughing Planet

Laughing Planet was the go-to spot for a vegetarian burrito in Bloomington for many years. College students used to frequent the burrito joint with a countercultural vibe by the popular Soma Cafe. The original owner who founded Laughing Planet in 1995 moved to Portland, where he opened a few more locations. The subsequent owner also owned Soma and Village Pantry down the street on Kirkwood Avenue. Bloomington's flagship Laughing Planet closed in 2021 because the owner was stretched too thin. The menu included Thai, green chile, and other vegetarian burritos made with tempeh, tofu, and black beans. It also had wraps, quesadillas, soups, salads, and bowls. It had a few chicken options but leaned heavily on vegan fare. Many people enjoyed their food outside on a patio watching the foot traffic pass by on Kirkwood.

Bamboo Inn

Bamboo Inn was long a destination for Asian cuisine on Monument Circle in downtown Indianapolis. The two-story Chinese American restaurant was located in the Circle Theatre building, where it operated from 1918 to 1961. It beckoned passersby with a large sign promising chop suey. The interior featured Chinese decor, an orchestra, and a bamboo balcony. It was acquired by the Tuen Hip Wey Association of Chicago in 1919, which brought in booth seating, cherry and marble finishings, and the addition of French cuisine and Club Orientale on the second floor. It later moved to the English Hotel and then Meridian Street.

Courtesy of Indiana Historical Society

Pie Pan

Courtesy of Freepik

Pie Pan Restaurant & Bakery in Evansville started serving diner fare in 1978. A homey spot that politicians stopped by when on the campaign trail, it aimed to "satisfy your hunger without cleaning out your wallet." The north side restaurant on North Park Drive served breakfast all day, as well as traditional American cuisine. As the name suggests, it was particularly well known for its freshly baked pies, which were available by the slice and à la mode. The apple, cherry, pumpkin, and pecan pies were particularly popular. It also baked other sweet treats like banana nut bread and chocolate chocolate chip muffins. It closed in 2024 after more than 40 years with the owners blaming the economy and the struggles small businesses faced.

Celebration Station

The billionaire Dean White established a billboard and motel empire around the country. He invested many of his proceeds back in Northwest Indiana, including at the Star Plaza Theatre and Radisson at Star Plaza hotel. He also opened the two-story Celebration Station in Merrillville in 1982. In the vein of ShowBiz Pizza and Prime Time Theatre, it was an amusement park with go-karts, a golf mountain, laser tag, batting cages, bumper boats, and an arcade centered around a Chuck-E-Cheese-like sit-down pizza restaurant. It featured the animatronic Harry Hound and his Band, which performed the "W.O.O.F. Radio" act with songs like a cover of Kool and the Gang's "Celebration" and a rendition of "Happy Birthday" at all the kids birthday parties that took place there. It adopted a Western saloon theme and added new animatronic characters over the years like the orangutan Buford and Jethro P. Hogg. In the 1990s, it brought in the Daniel and the Dixie Diggers band. Though it was the second to open, the Merrillville Celebration Station was the flagship in a chain where all the changes were first introduced. It still has a few locations left under different ownership in the South and West today. The curtains closed in Merrillville in 2001, but the old arcade tokens remain in circulation, periodically popping up on social media to trigger intense nostalgia.

Courtesy of Merrillville Historical Society

The White House

The White House in Valparaiso was less a seat of presidential power than a local landmark for 150 years. The Victorian-era mansion at East Jefferson Street and Morgan Boulevard was best known around town as a restaurant but had a longer, richer history. Valparaiso University President Henry Baker Brown built the 21-room, four-story house in about 1860 on Calkins Hill. It hosted prominent guests like President William Howard Taft, presidential candidate and Scopes Monkey Trial attorney William Jennings Bryan, and Irish President Éamon de Valera. The Pappas family opened a fine-dining restaurant in 1942 that served quail, prime rib, and shrimp-stuffed trout under chandeliers, including to celebrity visitors like Liberace and people marking special occasions like weddings and anniversaries. It closed in 1995, suffered a fire a few years later, was revived as a bridal shop and reception hall, and was eventually torn down to make way for condos.

Courtesy of *The Times of Northwest Indiana*

Flanagan's Restaurant & Pub

People flocked to Flanagan's Restaurant & Pub on Fort Wayne's southwest side for more than three decades. The casual eatery occupied a Victorian-style building in Covington Plaza on Covington Road. The Irish-themed pub served a few Irish items like bangers and mash, corned beef and cabbage, shepherd's pie, Irish stew, and a Guinness burger, making it a popular spot to celebrate St. Patrick's Day. But the extensive menu focused on American fare like burgers, steaks, seafood, pasta, flatbreads, salads, sandwiches, and wraps. The 150-seat eatery had a popular outdoor patio. It closed in 2017 when the owners retired and posted a sign on the door saying, "All Good Things Must Come to an End!" The similar but more modern Summit Grill Kitchen & Cocktails took over the space and carries on Flanagan's legacy as a gathering place for upscale but casual dinner and drinks.

Buggy Wheel

Courtesy of Wikimedia Commons

The Buggy Wheel Restaurant in Shipshewana fed visitors to Amish Country for more than two decades. The Mishler family, which owned the Bread Box Bakery & Cafe and Morton Street Bed and Breakfast, bought Troyer's Cafeteria in 1981 and rebranded it as the Buggy Wheel. It partnered with Ray's Coffee Co. and Big Olaf's Ice Cream to create the Morton Food Court. It served breakfast, lunch, and dinner, employing as many as 50 workers. The head count dwindled to six workers near the end, when it was reduced to a buffet and then a cafeteria-style operation. The restaurant ended up closing in 2006 after protracted struggles and the reopening of a nearby competitor, the Blue Gate Restaurant.

Courtesy of Sarah Stierch

Jim Dandy

If Jim Dandy reminded you of Big Boy, it was deliberate. The owners copied Big Boy's signature platter-touting mascot in coming up with their own cartoonish Jim Dandy figure, a blond-haired boy in overalls clutching a cheeseburger while licking his lips. The chain once had 11 locations in Central Indiana and closed its Noblesville diner in 2024 after 60 years. Only the Tipton restaurant remains. It started off as a drive-in with carhop service in 1964 and was so popular among cruisers in Noblesville it had to hire an off-duty policeman to direct traffic. It was especially known for its double burgers, broasted chicken, and coleslaw, which it also sold by the gallon. The owners estimate they sold more than 350,000 gallons of coleslaw over the decades.

Penguin Point

The Penguin Point fast-food chain started in Wabash in 1950 and spread across Northern Indiana and a few other states around the Midwest and South. It started out as a seasonal drive-in with carhops that was open only in the summer. Penguin Point focused on Wally Burgers, pork tenderloin sandwiches, and chicken sandwiches. It spread to locations across Northern Indiana, including Warsaw, Columbia City, and North Manchester. Texas-based US Assets took over in 2018 and made some changes, including adding breakfast fare. All the remaining locations closed in 2023.

Courtesy of The Indiana Album

Acapulco Joe's

Acapulco Joe's was one of the first Mexican restaurants in Central Indiana when it opened in 1960. The downtown Indianapolis restaurant introduced many residents to tacos, burritos, and other Mexican fare that later became mainstream, originally mixing in Mexican items to spice up a traditional diner menu. Every day at noon, it played "God Bless America." Owner Joe Rangel hailed from Guanajuato, was deported six times, and was even jailed for illegal immigration before gaining citizenship by marrying an American woman, but nonetheless he loved the country he first emigrated to at 13. He would turn the volume up so much on "God Bless America" that everyone had to quietly listen to it. Acapulco Joe's closed for good after then-owner Grant Redmond had his skull crushed in a violent attack outside in 2018 by a customer trying to skip out on a $50 bill. He survived; the long-running Mexican restaurant did not.

Courtesy of PoCo Muse

White House Restaurant

The White House Restaurant on Mishawaka Avenue and Twyckenham Drive in South Bend was better known as the 24-Hour Coffee Shop due to the bright neon sign reading that. Other nicknames included Fat Shirley's and the Gag and Heave. The no-frills diner served breakfast anytime. Customers sidled up to the counter, watching the cook prepare eggs, bacon, and sausage on the grill. They paid when served. The coffee flowed freely at the workingman's haunt. It was especially well-known for the Truckers' Special, which was also enjoyed by people who had been barhopping or went to punk shows at the Higher Ground. It was a dive some called "The Dirty Diner" and others characterized as "an icon of the South Bend late-night scene." It closed in 2009 after hitting the market and finding no buyer. One person fondly remembered it for "bottomless coffee, chain smoking, and greasy food with friends trying to sober up."

Courtesy of Jeanette Sawi

Santorini's

"Opa!" people would exclaim at Santorini's Greek Kitchen as saganaki was dramatically flambéed. Columns of fire would shoot up around the spacious dining room every few minutes. Santorini's was the spot to go for Greek food in Indianapolis until it closed in 2018 after nearly two decades when the owners suffered health problems. They still run the Santorini's Greek Kitchen Catering business in the Biltwell Event Center, occasionally hosting public buffets. The owners met in Santorini, Greece; emigrated to America two years later; and opened the popular dining spot in Fountain Square, which they called their baby. It served lamb, gyros, and other staples of Greek cuisine in a Mediterranean setting. It moved once and suffered a fire but remained a favorite, especially for its flaming cheese appetizer that made for fiery dinner theater.

Courtesy of St. Joseph Public Library

The Philadelphia

The Philadelphia was a downtown institution in South Bend for more than 70 years. The confectionary, soda fountain, restaurant, and bakery was opened in 1901 by Eustice Poledor. It was long run by the Poledor family. It catered to sweet tooths with items like an egg chocolate milkshake, a chocolate cashew sundae, and a raspberry ice cream soda that sold for 15 cents in the 1930s, according to the History Museum in South Bend. The restaurant focused on light lunch items like sandwiches, soups, and salads. It finally closed in 1972 when it was razed to make way for the city's downtown revitalization plan. A postcard claimed it was "known throughout the Middle West for Fine Candies, Food, and Ice Cream."

The Redwood Inn

The Redwood Inn was forever immortalized in the 1987 *New York Times* article "To Indianians (sic), if It's Not Hearty, It's Not Food." The restaurant was a favorite in Crawfordsville, the home of *Ben-Hur* author Gen. Lew Wallace and the tony all-boys private school Wabash College. The restaurant specialized in homestyle dishes like pork tenderloin, chicken fried steak, and chicken with homemade egg noodles over mashed potatoes. The paper of record described it as "real Indiana cooking" and "what was once daily fare in frontier Hoosier homes." It had a bakeshop that produced Finnish rye bread with anise seeds and the Hoosier classic sugar cream pie, which the Old Gray Lady described as "cloyingly sweet" but "to Indianians (sic), ambrosia itself."

Mudbugs

Mudbugs Cajun Café was a staple on Main Street in downtown Carmel for 13 years until it shuttered in late 2019, when the owners decided to retire. The restaurant served New Orleans–inspired dishes like catfish étouffée, shrimp po' boy sandwiches, and beignets dusted in powdered sugar. It won many fans with its hush puppies with a spicy rémoulade, which the Indiana State Fair named its signature food in 2007. While not known for its spicy cuisine, Central Indiana was at the time a hot spot for Cajun restaurants like the Yats chain and Broad Ripple's venerable Jazz Kitchen, as well as now-defunct favorites like B's Po Boy in Fountain Square, Papa Roux on the east side, Chef Dan's in Irvington, Borel's Cajun & Creole Cookery on the north side, SotSot Cajun Table on College Avenue, and Zydeco's in Mooresville.

Courtesy of Road Tips

Jonathan Byrd's

Seniors long flocked to Jonathan Byrd's cafeteria off Interstate 65 in Greenwood for fried chicken, mashed potatoes, and other traditional comfort food. KFC franchisees Jonathan and Ginny Byrd ran the quaint cafeteria, serving homestyle fare like meat loaf, potpies, and chicken and noodles for 26 years. Founded in 1988, it served millions of meals, cups of coffee, and slices of pie. Customers took a tray, walked down the 90-foot serving line, and loaded plates with their choice of more than 200 menu items, scooping food out of trays basking under heat lamps. The 400-seat cafeteria was a popular dining spot that sponsored the Indianapolis Colts and even had its own racing team in the Indianapolis 500. Longtime Sen. Richard Lugar campaigned outside during his last election. The spacious cafeteria closed in 2014, switching to a quick-serve model that closed two years later. Jonathan Byrd's lived on as a caterer in Carmel.

HOLLY HOUSE

The Holly House restaurant was a family-style diner on US 31 North in Roseland that opened in 1958, part of a chain run by Holly Grills. The 140-seat restaurant had a coffee shop, a snack bar, plenty of booths, and a cascading fountain with changing color patterns in the dining room. In 1972, the Michiana institution was taken over by Mike Bennitt and became known as Bennitt's Buffet. Tucked between a Pizza King and a laundromat and across from the lumber store, it served fare like frog legs until finally closing in the 1990s.

The Moderne Sweet Shop

Nicholas J. Kalamaros founded the Moderne Sweet Shop on Washington Street in downtown South Bend in 1929. It started out as a soda fountain and candy store. It was a classy establishment with a storefront adorned with Czechoslovakian stained glass, marble counters, and an ornately tiled floor. A soda jerk poured phosphates while rows of decadent candies beckoned from a glass case. In 1943, the Moderne added a restaurant serving lunch and dinner. One customer recalled that as a kid on a shopping trip downtown it was difficult to pass by all the delectable sweets while walking through the candy shop and soda fountain to the back where the restaurant's dining room was. The Kalamaros family ran it for 40 years until they sold it in 1967. It has since been razed and is now part of the Everwise Credit Union parking lot.

Courtesy of The History Museum, South Bend, Indiana

Courtesy of Freepik

Monon Restaurant

The restaurant was a favorite in Greencastle among both DePauw University students and townies for years. It was shut down in 2011 by the Indiana Department of Revenue after failing to pay its back retail taxes. It served homestyle cuisine like pork tenderloins, burgers, biscuits and gravy, and meat loaf Manhattans. "During its heyday, The Monon was one of those unique small-town eateries where a guy in a suit and tie was just as comfortable as the fellow in farm overalls and the mechanic in coveralls," wrote Eric Bernsee of the *Banner Graphic*. It hosted many characters, including a pastor who practiced his sermons in a booth and a businessman with a briefcase who carried on conversations with himself, often laughing loudly.

wplynn via Flickr

Milano Inn

The historic Milano Inn served traditional Italian fare on College Avenue east of downtown Indianapolis for 82 years. Joe and Mary Modaffari founded the Italian restaurant in 1934. It was nearly demolished in the 1980s but was saved by the LaGrotte family. It was a red sauce joint known for its pasta dishes, as well as artfully plated chicken piccata, bruschetta, and blackened tuna salad. It boasted decadent desserts like tiramisu and cannoli. Many celebrities stopped by, like Jim Nabors, Cowboy Bob, and Indy 500 race car drivers. The Milano Inn closed at the end of 2016 after Leo LaGrotte died. The South Bend–based developer Holladay Properties invested $4.5 million to redevelop the historic building into LaGrotte Square in honor of the longtime restaurateurs.

Courtesy of Freepik

Wooden Keg

The Wooden Keg on Main Street in South Bend used kegs as a design motif in tables, chairs, and coffee tables in the cozy bar area, which had a rustic vibe with stone walls, brick floors, and a stovetop. The elegant dining room had an aristocratic ambiance, offering fine dining with white tablecloths, linen napkins folded immaculately, and a mural with a family dinner after a fox hunt. Diners could enjoy candlelit dinners in the classy establishment, which imported fixtures from Europe. It offered first-class service like valet parking, cigarette girls, and violin players strolling around the dining room and serenading couples. The restaurant employed more than 60 employees at its height of popularity in the 1960s. It had two fishponds, a dance floor, and upscale cuisine like filet mignon. The Wooden Keg was tapped during the 1980s, officially dissolving in 1988.

Flakey Jake's

Flakey Jake's was a national chain with a popular location on Indianapolis's east side. The hamburger place drew comparisons to Fuddruckers, offering a more upscale experience than fast-food joints. Customers got a burger to order without toppings and went to a dress-it-yourself bar where they could add whatever condiments and veggies they wanted. The gourmet burger restaurant ground all its ground beef and baked its buns in-house. Its bakery also made cinnamon rolls and other goodies customers could take home. The Seattle-based chain had more than 50 restaurants in the 1980s but went out of business by the 1990s. Red Robin, a similar gourmet burger restaurant, moved into many of its former locations. Fuddruckers, which sued Flakey's over copying its concept, is still around despite financial troubles.

Courtesy of Freepik

Empress Court

Empress Court provided Chinese cuisine to Bedford for nearly three decades. Henry and Sarah Wong and her father, Guo Zhang, opened the restaurant in 1994. Empress Court prepared traditional dishes like kung pao chicken, pepper steak, cashew chicken, twice-cooked pork, and moo shu pork. It closed in 2021 as a result of surging food prices, difficulty finding employees, and trouble renewing the lease under favorable terms. The owners had a month-to-month lease and did not feel comfortable committing to three years with all the operational challenges they faced, having tired of working 12 hours a day every single day.

The Iron Skillet

The Iron Skillet on Indianapolis's west side specialized in pan-fried chicken, as the name suggests. The old-school restaurant opened in an old farmhouse on a sprawling 80-acre property that had previously been used as a clubhouse at 2489 West 30th Street in 1953. For more than 70 years, it served home-cooked food like steak, walleye, pike, shrimp, and the skillet-fried chicken in family-style portions. The shared meals were huge, with sides like mashed potatoes, green beans, corn, cottage cheese, beets, salad, and biscuits with apple butter. Diners relished the ice cream, which was topped with chocolate, butterscotch, creme de menthe, and strawberry sauces. Owner Ronald Torr shuttered the eatery in 2024 after turning 74 years old and tiring of the hassle of a nearby bridge construction project.

The Lido Supper Club

The Lido Supper Club at 127 North Main Street in downtown South Bend was a classy establishment with velvet booths, credenzas, and telephone service with a phone jack at every table. Previously a saloon known as Club Lido, it was located in a downtown building that later became home to the popular Fiddler's Hearth pub, a traditional Irish public house with frequent live music acts. It faced some labor troubles, including when the local bartenders' and waitresses' union picketed outside in 1964. The high-end eatery served steak, lobster, frog legs, whole dover sole, escargot, and flaming desserts like cherries jubilee, as well as an extensive cocktail menu. It was a classy establishment that often hosted proms. It closed in the 1980s after supper clubs fell out of favor.

Snooty Fox

The Snooty Fox had a nearly 30-year run in Indianapolis's north-side Nora neighborhood. It was a British-style pub with a wide-ranging menu that featured steaks, seafood, pasta, burgers, salads, and other largely American cuisine in an old-school setting with a "plaid Hunt Club look," as *Indianapolis Monthly* put it. It started to struggle to attract younger customers and signed up for season 2 of the Food Network's *Restaurant: Impossible* in 2011. Chef Robert Irvine came in and overhauled it, giving it a chalkboard menu focus with more actual English cuisine. Despite the glamorous revamp, it closed later that year.

Charlie's Drive-In

bballchico via Flickr

When Charlie's Drive-In first opened in Martinsville, it cost 15 cents for a Coney dog, 10 cents for popcorn, and 10 cents for a root beer or an orange pop. The longtime institution shuttered after 67 years in Martinsville in 2020. Owners Ed and Vicky Littell took it over in 2010, aimed to keep it open for another 10 years, and did just that. It's where Vicky worked her whole life, where Ed first asked her if he could walk her home, and where he proposed to her in her favorite booth. They told the *Martinsville Reporter-Times* their children spent as much time there as they did at home. Many regulars also frequented the place over the generations.

Hammer's Food & Drink

The boxer Kenny Larson ran Hammer's restaurant on US 20 in Michigan City for decades. His father, the former sailor Roger Larson, ran Roger's Chow-Mein in Minneapolis before coming to Northwest Indiana to manage the Red Lantern Inn in Beverly Shores, where he cut his teeth in the business. Kenny became known as the Lafayette Hammer when winning the Indiana Golden Gloves Tournament in 1981. He went on to box professionally and then ran restaurants like Pumps Pasta and Pizza. He realized a longtime dream by founding the 130-seat restaurant Hammer's, which punched up the menu with boxing terms. The made-from-scratch menu included steak, ribs, lake perch, pasta, pizza, and sandwiches. The walls were lined with photos from Kenny's boxing days as well as of notable visitors like Larry King and the University of Southern California football team.

PJ Chmiel via Flickr

Honey Creme Donut Shop

People went to the Honey Creme Donut Shop in New Albany for 80 years. The family-owned doughnut shop started in the mid-1940s, serving countless early-morning regulars, generations of customers and families that passed on the tradition of grabbing a sackful of doughnuts there. Apple fritters and glazed doughnuts were especially popular among customers who often had been going there since they were kids. It was such an institution that a street sign marked the neighboring alley as Donut Alley. In recent years, the small brick building was covered by an Art Cartel mural that featured an anthropomorphic doughnut with a chunk bitten out of its hide giving a thumbs-up and honeycombs and bees resembling the Honey Nut Cheerios mascot. The owners tried to auction off the doughnut shop in late 2024 and ended up closing it in early 2025.

Carriage Inn

Based out of a quaint Victorian home, the Carriage Inn baked pizza for residents of Tell City and greater Perry County for 41 years. It also served pasta, submarine sandwiches, salads, and homemade desserts like cupcakes. Some standouts included the Aloha Burger, PB and No J Burger, and the Shaver with thinly sliced steak. Located right in downtown Tell City, the Carriage Inn had a cozy tavern-like atmosphere with brick walls, wood paneling, a fireplace, and various beer signs adorning the walls. It closed during the COVID-19 pandemic in 2020 after the owners couldn't get a grant or a loan.

Rocky's
Sub Pub

Darrell Harden via Flickr

Rocky's Sub Pub was a mainstay on the Ohio River in Jeffersonville for more than four decades. The Southern Indiana restaurant served sub sandwiches, calzones, pizza, and other casual Italian fare for 42 years. Founder John Fondrisi made pasta, calamari, and other traditional dishes from scratch with classic Italian recipes. Rocky's started out on Market Street in 1977 and moved to the waterfront, becoming a gathering place during big events like the Thunder Over Louisville fireworks show. Its outdoor patio offered sweeping views of Louisville's skyline and bridges. It boasted 20 televisions, 32 beers on tap, and what it claimed was the best view of Louisville's downtown. It was replaced by the Jefferson music venue after it closed in 2018.

The Pines

The Pines shuttered in the Ohio River town of Madison in 2019 after nearly four decades. Owners Mary Beth Hamilton and Mike Hall decided to close the southern Indiana staple, which specialized in down-home fare, because they wanted to retire. The buffet was known for hearty cuisine like fried chicken, fried fish, roast beef, ribs, ham, mac and cheese, and mashed potatoes. A favorite was the prime rib, which came with horseradish on the side. It had Friday night seafood buffets during Lent. A staple many regulars visited since childhood, the Pines had a catering business and banquet hall. It was replaced by the Mi Viejo Mexican restaurant, which also had a location in Carrollton, Kentucky.

Clarksville Seafood

Clarksville Seafood on Eastern Boulevard in Clarksville offered a fresh catch just off the banks of the Ohio River. It opened in the 1960s. A favorite of the wrestling promoter and podcaster Jim Cornette, the small fish house was a descendent of the Cape Codder chain that was owned in part by KFC founder Colonel Harland Sanders. Customers came up to the counter to place an order for fried fish, clams, shrimp, or other seafood, which came in baskets with sides like coleslaw and hush puppies. There was a bubbling fish tank in the waiting area, along with a life preserver, a "some true fish stories told here" sign, and other nautical decor. It was eventually acquired by Hubert Rockey, the owner of Dock Seafood in neighboring Jeffersonville. It closed not long after he died.

Courtesy of Freepik

Courtesy of Freepik

Mr. Happy Burger

Mr. Happy Burger started in Logansport in 1961 and ended up in the Indiana Restaurant Association's Indiana Restaurant Hall of Fame. Bob "Haps" Shanks founded the business at a time when fast-food restaurants were taking off and was known for greeting guests with a positive attitude. He sold the business at the age of 89, telling the *Pharos-Tribune* he needed to slow down. Mr. Happy Burger was featured in Kevin Rader's *Only in Indiana* series on WTHR in Indianapolis. Nicknamed Haps around town, it was sandwiched between McDonald's and Burger King. It maintained a 1950s and 1960s ambiance. It first sold a burger, fries, and milkshake for 45 cents, locally sourcing its corn-fed beef. It displayed a cow statue out front, which many stopped to take pictures by. Shanks eventually sold Mr. Happy Burger to the Penguin Point Restaurant Group so he could retire, and it later closed.

Wimpy

Wimpy, the notorious moocher in the Popeye cartoons, always proclaimed he would gladly pay you Tuesday for a hamburger today. Wimpy was founded in Bloomington in 1934. It expanded across the Midwest, including arriving in 1936 in Chicago, where it would establish a large footprint. Ten of its 26 stores in six states were in the Chicagoland metro, such as at the massive Woodfield Mall in Schaumburg. Wimpy grew into a multinational business in 1954, reaching 1,500 locations across the globe. It had 500 restaurants in the United Kingdom where it was protested over a policy banning unescorted women between midnight and 6 a.m. Wimpy still has a presence in South Africa, but all the US restaurants closed after Gold died in 1977.

Courtesy of Wikimedia Commons

Mac's Hideaway

Mac's Hideaway was a Southern Indiana nightlife spot for nearly a quarter century. The sports bar and grill on Slate Run Road in New Albany just across from Louisville closed after 24 years in 2025 because of a forthcoming rent hike. It specialized in fried fish but served other New American pub fare like pork tenderloin, pizza, grilled chicken salads, chicken bacon ranch quesadillas, and, of course, burgers. Burgers were a house specialty that were served with toasted buns. Many went there to watch a game or take part in the popular Kentuckiana Trivia Night. It had live bands, DJs, karaoke, and pool. It was best known around town as a laid-back hangout spot where the cheap drinks flowed freely.

Courtesy of Freepik

Bon Femme

Bon Femme was a destination for French cuisine in the Calumet Region. The upscale restaurant opened in 1977 and long operated in Merrillville before moving to Lincolnway in downtown Valparaiso, taking over the former Clayton's space in 2005. Keith Gurley, who cut his teeth at Angelo's Sicilian Cart in Merrillville, took over the place, buying it after owner George Nissan originally bought it. In addition to French fare, it served steaks, seafood, and salads. The fine-dining spot, a favorite for date nights, used top-notch ingredients like organic grass-fed beef. The ever-changing menu often featured new specials. Bon Femme displayed French country decor but tried to deflate its image of sophistication by not taking itself too seriously, greeting guests with large paintings of cows. It ended up closing after four decades and was rebranded as the Southern-themed Fork & Cork.

Courtesy of Freepik

Courtesy of The Indiana Album

Cafe Johnell

Cafe Johnell has been called "arguably the most elegant restaurant ever located in Fort Wayne." The restaurant on South Calhoun Street opened in the 1960s, preparing fine French food that First Lady Jacqueline Kennedy had popularized. John N. Spillson launched the upscale, award-winning restaurant some claimed was "one of the finest in the Midwest." It maintained a four-star rating in national restaurant guides for 25 straight years. Cafe Johnell was a classy establishment with linen tablecloths, red-velvet upholstery, and an extensive wine cellar. The decor included antiques, paintings, and freshly cut flowers. The family-owned restaurant was a destination for date nights for 40 years until it closed in 2001.

Captain Alexander's Wharf/Moonraker

Captain Alexander's Wharf/Moonraker was started by the restaurateur Alex Azar in Fort Wayne in 1978. It grew to other locations, including in South Bend, where it was located on the east bank of the St. Joseph River across from the Century Center. The Davey's Locker disco was upstairs. The space was later taken over by the South Bend Brewery. The menu included shrimp, fish, crab legs, lobster, and other seafood, such as a Captain's Platter sampler. It had a Singapore Oyster Bar. Azar, the son of Syrian immigrants who started out in the grocery business after serving in World War II, owned several other restaurants like Big Boy drive-ins and Roby's Roast Beef, which Marriott acquired and rebranded as Roy Rogers, still a popular chain in the Northeast.

Courtesy of Freepik

Poe's Cafeteria

After feeding generations hearty, homestyle fare, Poe's Cafeteria closed in Martinsville in 2003 and then in Mooresville in 2019. Both times, the local newspaper dubbed it the "end of an era." Bill and Barbara Poe opened the traditional café in 1954 in Martinsville, serving down-home dishes and homemade pies with often unusual flavors like gooseberry and strawberry rhubarb. It started on the north side of the Morgan County Courthouse Square, hopped over to the south side, and then moved to Indiana 37 to capture passing highway traffic. It displayed local history on the walls and had a wall of fame highlighting local celebrities like Coach John Wooden. It expanded to Mooresville in 1982. The last remaining location in Mooresville closed for good when the Poe family finally decided to retire.

THEME RESTAURANTS

Circle Centre Mall in downtown Indianapolis used to have a Planet Hollywood, the gaudy, over-the-top type of theme restaurant that was popular in the 1990s. The horseshoe-themed Colts Grille fed fans nearby. Indiana remains home to many novel themed restaurants, like the factorylike Industrial Revolution in Valparaiso with a metal sculpture over the entrance that replicates the famous photo of steelworkers perched atop a skyscraper beam. Fairmount's Grains and Grill is in an old grain and feed building, and Richmond's Firehouse BBQ and Blues occupies an old firehouse. Theme restaurants have largely fallen out of favor, but Indiana had some memorable ones.

Tin Star

Courtesy of Freepik

People used to dine in booths in jail cells in the Tin Star in Indianapolis's Broad Ripple neighborhood. The "jail restaurant" on 62nd Street and Keystone had the slogan "Where the Roast Beef and Baked Ham Sandwiches Are Wanted for Great Taste!" Originally called John's Jail, the Tin Star specialized in roast beef sandwiches. The menu also included fries, cherry Cokes, and salads that regulars described as delicious but fattening. Some patrons claimed it had the best pork tenderloin in the Circle City. It also had a location on Pennsylvania and Market Streets downtown, which had jail cells down in the basement. It was especially popular with kids until it closed in 2005.

Illusions

Dinner and a show usually means dinner theater, but at Illusions in Carmel it meant tableside magic acts. Customers had to pull a sword out of a stone to enter. Each waiter performed magic tricks while checking on customers and taking orders. Magicians also did their acts in the lounge. The magic-themed restaurant hosted magicians like Eugene Burger, Michael Close, Charles Greene III, Chris Kenner, and Homer Liwag. It was an especially popular place to go for birthday parties. The magic ran out when it closed in 2003 after more than a decade. Some of the displaced magicians went on to form Indy Magic Monthly, performing at venues around town.

Courtesy of Carmel-Clay Historical Society

Courtesy of Freepik

The Caves 'N Cavern

Diners could spelunk into a unique dining experience at the Caves 'N Cavern in Indianapolis's Nora neighborhood. People ate inside artificial caves and caverns in the Caves 'N Cavern restaurant. Part of the Sam's Subway Restaurant Group that included sub shops around Indy, the theme restaurant was located in Northview Mall on 86th Street at the tony northern edge of the city. The menu included steak, ribs, and seafood such as trout, shrimp, and crab legs that customers consumed in a labyrinth of rock formations. Diners also could fill up at the salad and soup bar. It had the slogans "enough to conquer the heartiest appetite" and "where sophisticated cave people meet to eat" and a logo depicting a cavewoman dragging a caveman she had just clubbed.

Tee Pee Restaurants

Courtesy of Indiana Landmarks

Indianapolis's Tee Pee Restaurants were unmistakable because each had a large teepee on the top of its roof. Tee Pee was launched on Fall Creek Parkway in the 1930s as a combination dine-in, take-out, and drive-in concept. Aiming to lure customers during the Great Depression, it was open nearly round the clock to cater to diners at all hours. It served burgers, steaks, seafood, and pie for dessert. It enjoyed a height of popularity after World War II when drive-ins became popular hangout spots. It opened a few more locations on the south side and Nora. But drive-ins eventually lost favor to fast food, and Tee Pee closed all its locations in the 1980s.

Northwoods

Northwoods Hearty Home Cookin' & Saloon whipped up hearty homestyle fare like meat loaf, pot roast, and fireside chili in St. John. The lodge hosted countless live music acts over the years, serving as one of the most popular venues for local bands in Northwest Indiana, like the Nomad Planets and the Crawpuppies. The supper-club-style restaurant inspired by the Wisconsin Northwoods near Michigan's Upper Peninsula occupied a giant, rustic, rough-hewn log cabin on a heavily trafficked stretch of US 41 near Lake Central High School. Modeled after a similar restaurant in nearby Crete, Illinois, it sat up to 450 diners in a 15,000-square-foot lodge on a 9.3-acre site with a pond, waterfall, and sprawling patio. The high operating costs led it to close in 2013 and sit vacant for years. The owners of the local Coffee Cabin chain revived it in 2021, but it closed in 2024.

BARS AND BREWERIES

Indiana has many legendary watering holes, like Nick's English Hut, Kilroy's, Harry's Chocolate Shop, Fiddler's Hearth, the Melody Inn, and Union Jack Pub, where countless stories of youthful revelry took place. It's home to touristy pubs like the Slippery Noodle Inn, the state's oldest bar and a popular live blues venue, and neighborhood dive bars like the He Ain't Here Lounge in Lake Station. In Indy, one can imbibe in the historic Rathskeller biergarten, the homey Broad Ripple Tavern, or the St. Joseph Brewery in an old Catholic church. The state boasts renowned breweries like 3 Floyds, Sun King, and Upland. But many Hoosier bars and breweries did not survive Prohibition. Others just eventually fizzled out.

Courtesy of the Irish Lion

Irish Lion

Generations of Indiana University students drank, dined, and hung out at the Irish Lion. The longtime Irish pub on Kirkwood Avenue downtown started out as a pub and inn in 1882. Early settler Zimri McCollough opened the Worley Tavern and Hotel Bundy European upstairs. The building hosted many different taverns and pool halls over the years, until it was acquired by the McConnaughy family, who opened the Irish Lion there in 1982. The wood-paneled pub oozed Celtic ambiance, poured Guinness, and served traditional Irish fare like corned beef, shepherd's pie, and bangers and mash. But the longtime owners opted to retire in 2024, and the restaurant became delivery only.

Courtesy of the Irish Lion

TERRE HAUTE BREWING COMPANY

The Terre Haute Brewing Company was Indiana's oldest and America's second oldest brewery. Chauncey Warren and Demas Deming Sr. founded the brewery in 1837, inspiring the slogan "Breaking the Law since 1837." It expanded when the German immigrant Anton Mayer bought it and took over as brewmaster. It sprawled across two city blocks and made 30,000 barrels a day by 1880. By the turn of the century, it was America's seventh-largest brewery with a production capacity of 100,000 barrels a day. It became known for its flagship Champagne Velvet beer, which it brewed a nonalcoholic breakfast version of to make it through Prohibition. Terre Haute Brewing Company distributed its beers nationally by 1935, when it installed the largest brewing line ever constructed. The brewery was sold and moved to Chicago in 1958. The Terre Haute Brewing Company name has since been resurrected as a modern-day craft brewery decades after the original brewery closed.

Courtesy of Vigo County History Center

Scotty's Brewhouse

Founded outside Ball State University in Muncie in 1996, Scotty's Brewhouse grew into a popular chain of brewpubs around Indianapolis and in college towns around the state. It was a laid-back place to hang out, swig craft beer, and enjoy American cuisine. Scotty's Brewhouse had locations in Muncie, Bloomington, Mishawaka, Brownsburg, Fort Wayne, Noblesville, and Indianapolis, as well as a few in Illinois, Ohio, Florida, and Texas. The expansive menu was designed to resemble an issue of *Sports Illustrated*. It included pizza, burgers, mussels, fried pickles, tater tot nachos, and other American cuisine. It was especially known for its specialty burgers, including the peanut- butter-topped Shewman Burger. It poured craft beer brewed by Three Wise Men Brewing Co., a brewery it started in Broad Ripple. The chain folded after filing for bankruptcy in 2018.

Courtesy of the *Indiana Daily Student*

Brugge Brasserie

Brugge Brasserie was an early pioneer in Indy's craft beer scene and a destination in its trendy Broad Ripple neighborhood for more than 15 years. The Belgian gastropub was on the Monon Trail, where many people sat outside on the patio to enjoy duck confit sandwiches, mussels, frites, and the highly potent Tripel de Ripple. Many would contend there was no better way to spend a summer day than sipping Tripel while dipping their frites in various ramekins of aioli and other sauces while watching cyclists, joggers, and walkers pass by. The brewpub shuttered during the coronavirus pandemic in 2020 and is often cited as one of the most missed restaurants in the Circle City. The owners were still hoping to reopen somewhere new as of 2025.

Courtesy of Brugge Brasserie

MacNiven's

Some claimed MacNiven's Restaurant and Bar on Massachusetts Avenue in Indianapolis was the best place in the Midwest for vegetarian haggis. The Scottish restaurant and bar also was well known for its regular haggis, a sheep's heart, liver, and lung boiled inside its stomach along with oatmeal, onion, suet, spices, and stock. Many consider the very idea of the dish to be unappetizing, but the adventurous sought it out as a bucket-list item to try at least once. One of the anchors of the Mass Ave Cultural Arts District after it opened in 2003, MacNiven's served other authentic Scottish cuisine like beans on toast, neeps, mince and tatties, steak pie, sausage rolls, fish and chips, and of course Scotch eggs. The festive pub ambiance made it a great place to watch soccer. It closed in 2020 to make way for the new seafood concept called Raw Bar, an extension of Slapfish.

Elbow Room

Elbow Room Pub & Deli was an institution in downtown Indianapolis for more than 80 years. The bar and restaurant occupied a distinctive wedge-shaped building that resembled New York City's famed Flatiron Building. The building at 602 North Pennsylvania Street was constructed in 1893, and the Elbow Room opened there in 1933, just after Prohibition was repealed. Previously home to Schoen Brothers Cleaners, it was a chill hangout spot with darts, pool, arcade games like Big Buck Hunter, and sweeping views of the streetscape from the second-floor windows. A neon-lit Elbow Room sign beckoned patrons off the street to the old-school wooden bar. It served standard pub fare and relatively cheap drinks even as downtown gentrified around it with an influx of IUPUI students and young people before it closed in 2017.

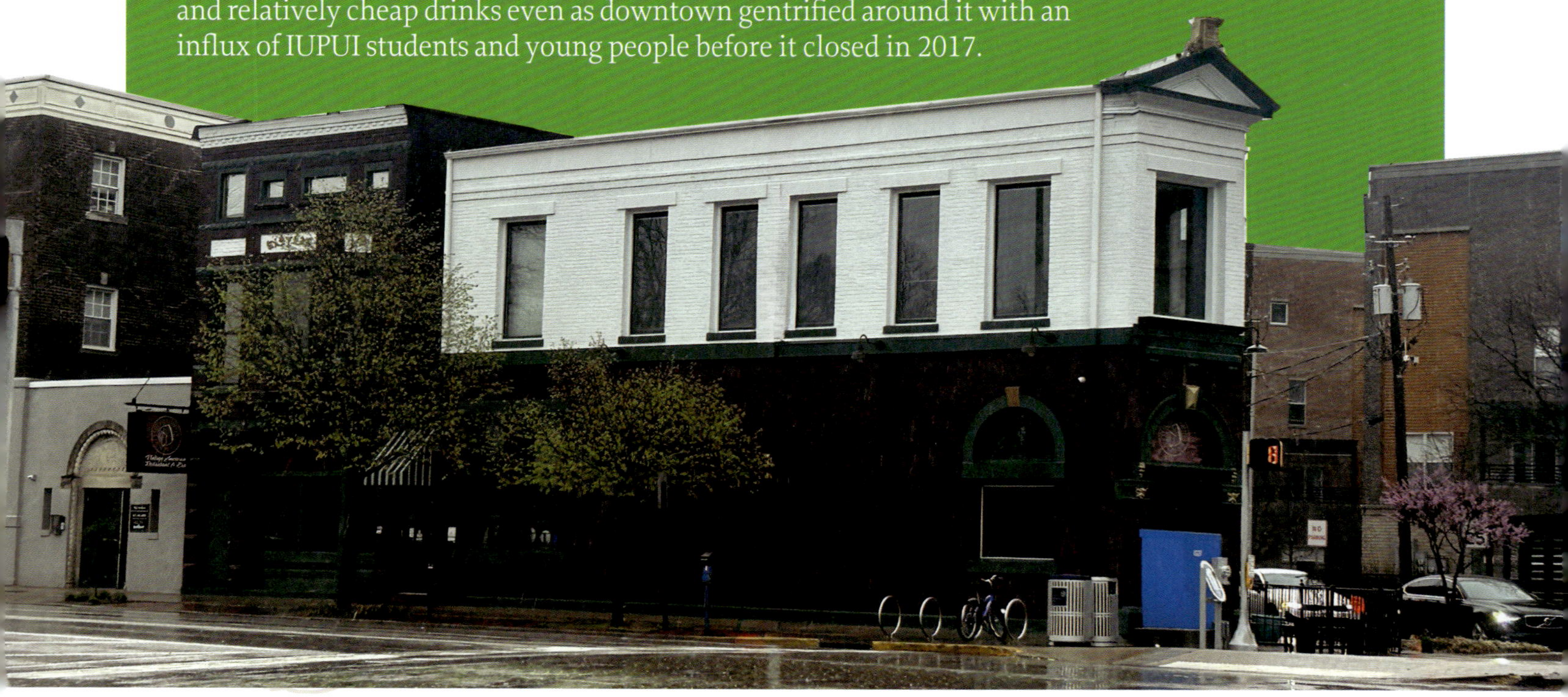

Old Point Tavern

The angular Old Point Tavern first occupied a prominent corner on Massachusetts Avenue in 1887, remaining there until the 21st century. The old-school tavern was Indianapolis's second-oldest bar after the Slippery Noodle Inn. Once serving boardinghouse customers from upstairs, it remained a steady vestige of the past even as the neighborhood changed. The kinetic neon *Ann Dancing* sculpture was parked outside, forever swaying to a silent rhythm. Decorated with paintings of the Three Stooges and Richard Pryor, it was a popular spot to drink and dine alfresco in the summer while the world passed by on the Indianapolis Cultural Trail outside. Favorites included the nachos, chili, and half pints. Patti and Chic Perrin ran it from 1990 until they retired in 2018, selling to the Cunningham Restaurant Group. It's now Tavern at the Point, an elevated gastropub that's a far cry from the original dive bar.

NICKEL PLATE
Bar and Grill

People flocked for nearly three decades to Nickel Plate Bar and Grill in Fishers for dinner or drinks. The eatery in a historic 1880s building closed in 2019 after 28 years to make way for a $157 million Nickel Plate District downtown development project. Nickel Plate Bar and Grill sat on East 116th Street just off the railroad corridor that slices through the downtown of the fast-growing suburb. It was previously home to the Parks Place Saloon. It was famed for its giant pork tenderloin sandwiches, but the menu also included burgers and other pub fare. With its brick walls, it was an oasis of authentic old-town character in a suburb filled with glistening new subdivisions. It was a favorite in town but also a regional destination, as it was one of the few Pittsburgh Steelers bars in the Indy area.

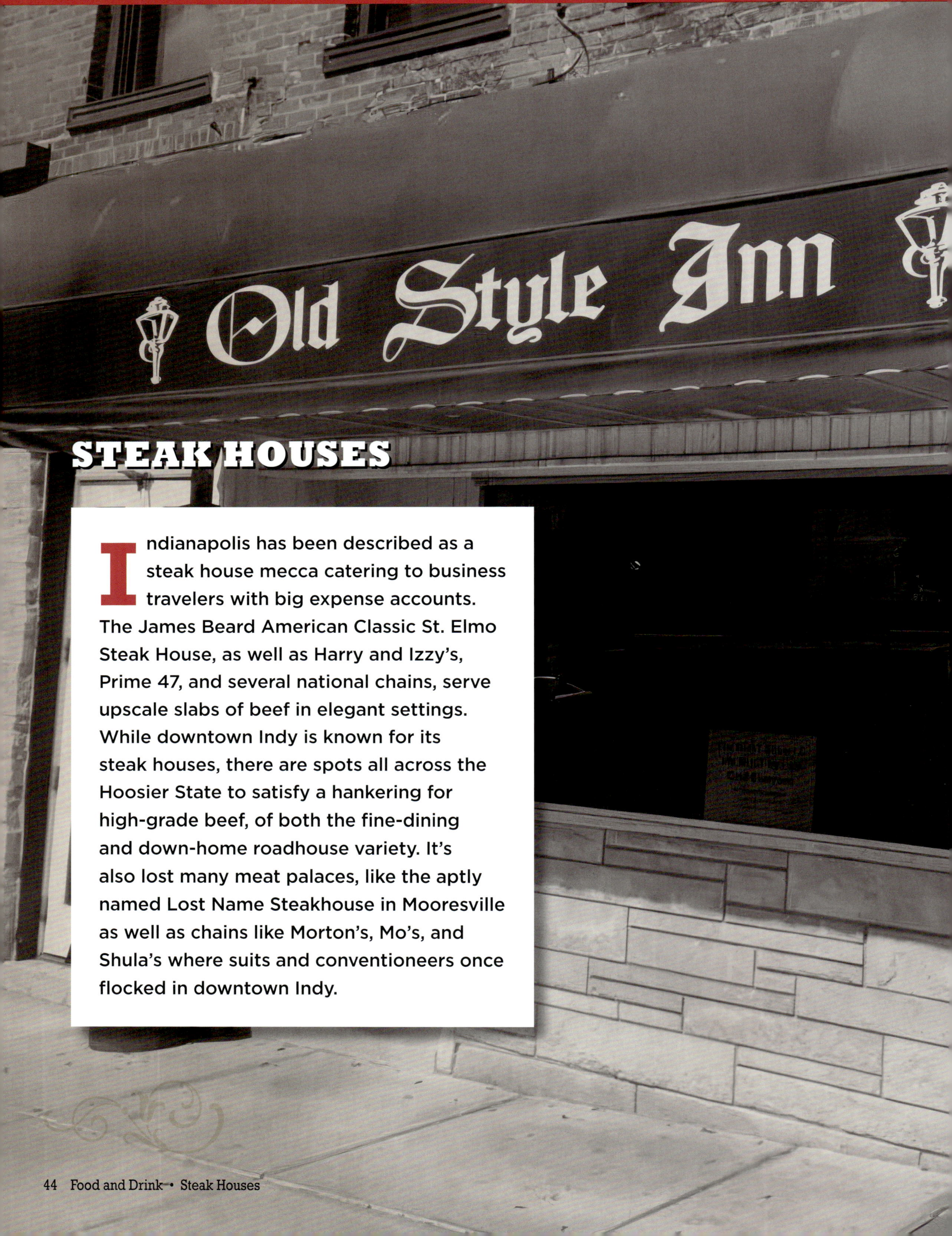

STEAK HOUSES

Indianapolis has been described as a steak house mecca catering to business travelers with big expense accounts. The James Beard American Classic St. Elmo Steak House, as well as Harry and Izzy's, Prime 47, and several national chains, serve upscale slabs of beef in elegant settings. While downtown Indy is known for its steak houses, there are spots all across the Hoosier State to satisfy a hankering for high-grade beef, of both the fine-dining and down-home roadhouse variety. It's also lost many meat palaces, like the aptly named Lost Name Steakhouse in Mooresville as well as chains like Morton's, Mo's, and Shula's where suits and conventioneers once flocked in downtown Indy.

Old Style Inn

Diners feasted on prime rib at Old Style Inn in downtown Valparaiso for 85 years. The staple of the thriving downtown Valpo dining scene opened in 1932 on the Porter County Courthouse Square. It was an upscale place where couples went for a night out on the town or to celebrate special occasions. Diners feasted on steaks, pasta, duck, crab legs, and all-you-can-eat lake perch in an old-school ambiance with wood-paneled walls that some compared to longtime institutions on Chicago's South Side. It served its signature prime rib daily. Its clientele aged as it did, and it went out of business in 2017. Peddlers Pizza Pub moved into the historic brick building.

Courtesy of Steve Shook

Palomino

Palomino Restaurant & Bar was a classy dining destination in the Circle Centre Mall in downtown Indianapolis that closed in 2019. The fancy, upscale restaurant at 49 West Maryland Street specialized in European fare, including steak and frites, artisan pizzas, and craft cocktails. It had been open for 23 years, nearly as long as the mall itself, which suffered many closures before a redevelopment project kicked off in 2025. Palomino was one of many street-level restaurants at the mall, like Rock Bottom Brewery and Primanti Brothers, that have since faded from the scene. It was part of a small Seattle-based chain that had been around for 30 years. It was owned by Restaurants Unlimited, a restaurant group that also owned Cutters Crabhouse, Henry's Tavern, Manzana Grill, and Skates on the Bay. It filed for bankruptcy in 2019 and was purchased by Landry's.

Nikchick via Flickr. creativecommons.org/licenses/by-sa/2.0/deed.en

Dunaway's Palazzo Ossigeno

The singer-songwriter John Mellencamp once took Meg Ryan, whom he dated for a few years, to Dunaway's Palazzo Ossigeno in Indianapolis for her birthday, flying her out when he was in town performing at Clowes Memorial Hall. The place at 351 South East Street had arguably the best rooftop dining in Indianapolis, with a sweeping view of the skyline. Former St. Elmo co-owner Jeff Dunaway opened the fine-dining restaurant in 1998. It was a classy establishment with candelabras in its dark-paneled Fireplace Room. It at one point employed the former chef to Tiger Woods. The high-end menu included steaks, chops, scallops, fingerling potatoes, horseradish mashed potatoes, crab cakes, a caprese tower, and goat cheese salad with cabernet-poached beets. It closed in late 2014.

Courtesy of *The Times of Northwest Indiana*

Country Lounge

The swanky Country Lounge was a staple in Hobart for 70 years before it closed in 2013. The upscale Hobart institution at 3700 Montgomery Street was originally known as Hunky Hollow in the 1960s and 1970s, when it was a bustling destination. It had a Sinatra-esque vibe and a sophisticated menu that included broiled steaks, seafood, chicken, and pasta. Popular items included steak Diane, prime rib, lake perch, crab legs, oysters Rockerfeller, and its popular shrimp de Jonghe. It was a place where politicians, power brokers, bankers, and businesspeople cut deals while the cocktails flowed freely. It became known as the New Country Lounge after longtime customers bought it in 2011, but it didn't last much longer under the new ownership.

DINERS AND DRIVE-INS

Guy Fieri of the popular show *Diners, Drive-Ins and Dives* has made pit stops at more than a dozen Indiana locations, like Steer-In in Indianapolis, Triple XXX in West Lafayette, and the South Side Soda Shop and Diner in Goshen. Indiana also has many vintage drive-ins, like the Blue Top in Highland, Carlson's in Michigan City, and the Port in Chesterton, that offer a classic taste of 1950s car culture. Some even still have waitresses on roller skates bringing out orders. Indiana also has time-capsule diners like Plainfield's Oasis Diner that's in an original 1954 Mountain View Diner from Singac, New Jersey. But such old-school dining experiences where the coffeepot is always on and the jukebox is hopping are fewer and farther between these days.

Courtesy of the Library of Congress

The Huddle Restaurants

Indianapolis once had five Huddle Restaurants, 24/7 diners that slung coffee, breakfast fare, and USDA Choice steak. The home of the Wimpy and the Old Farm Breakfast also had locations in Bloomington, Fort Wayne, Terre Haute, and Marion. Often attached to Haag drugstores, they offered breakfast staples like omelets and pancakes all day as well as the usual diner menu of burgers, club sandwiches, and salads. Dinner included seafood and steaks. An Edward Hopper–esque refuge for night owls, the diners were popular in the 1950s and 1960s. People often sidled into the vinyl booths after late nights at the bar for some greasy hash browns and bottomless pots of coffee. Many were located near nightclubs. The last one closed in 1976.

HALL'S
Original Drive-In

Hall's Original Drive-In had a run of 75 years in Fort Wayne. The family-owned restaurant was a popular spot for cruisers to swing by in the 1950s and was visited by generations of Fort Wayne residents. It served burgers, fries, frosties, and fast-food fare like the Big Buster platter. It also served breakfast and was especially popular on weekends. Don Hall founded the family-owned restaurant at 1502 Bluffton Road in Quimby Village. Diners inundated the vintage joint in 2021 to get one last taste before it closed forever. The Hall family still owns 10 other restaurants around Fort Wayne, including Hall's Hollywood, the Factory, and the Gas House.

Courtesy of Allen County Public Library

Riley Park Drive-In

In the 1930s, Link Fair at Fair's Lunch in Greenfield invented the Wet Tenderloin, a spin on the pork tenderloin that's Indiana's official state sandwich. Gerald "Whitey" Ware helped Fair perfect the gravy and took the recipe over to Riley Park Drive-In, which Ware went on to manage, said Brigette Cook Jones, board member and past president of the Hancock County Historical Society. The drive-in by Riley Park eventually changed its name to Jim Dandy, an Indiana chain that was a popular teen hangout in the 1950s and 1960s but that's now down to one location. Jim Dandy would go on to trademark the phrase Wet Tenderloin. "Other restaurants could serve it, but they couldn't call it a Wet Tenderloin," Jones said. The restaurant moved to State Street in 1983 and closed as a result of COVID. It's now a florist shop.

Courtesy of the Hancock County Historical Society

Courtesy of the *Indiana Daily Student*

WAFFLE HOUSE

Bloomington's Waffle House restaurant was originally affiliated with but ultimately parted ways with the well-known Southern chain of short-order diners that glow like *Nighthawks* at the Art Institute of Chicago and are so reliably open 24/7 that FEMA has a "Waffle House Index" to chart the severity of storms. This Waffle House was also a diner but a stand-alone one on North College Avenue that was torn down in 2013 after 46 years to make room for luxury apartments. Countless IU students of varying degrees of sobriety sidled into the vinyl booths for eggs, bacon, and other greasy breakfast fare. The second-oldest Bloomington restaurant after Nick's English Hut, it opened in 1967. It was always open save for Christmas Day, serving breakfast at all hours. It catered to a mix of students, seniors, and regulars who didn't need to glance at the laminated menus to know what they would order.

GARDNER'S Drive-In/Char-King

Courtesy of the Allen County Public Library

Gardner's Drive-In started out as a walk-up root beer stand with 11 seats in 1935. Owner Frank Gardner soon expanded the Fort Wayne restaurant at Jefferson and Webster into a larger drive-in that was known for its burgers and frosted malts. He went on to found the sit-down Colonial Restaurant that offered a more formal dining experience and Char-King, a burger joint that grew to three locations, including across from the Fort Wayne Coliseum. Char-King was known for its burgers, fried chicken, fried seafood, fountain drinks, hot fudge sundaes, and pies, such as its famed pecan cream pie. One could wash it all down with phosphates, ginger ale, orange ale, lemon ale, or lime ale. Waitresses brought the food right out to one's car. Char-King reached the end of the road in 1971, when Gardner sold the restaurants.

Peppy Grill

Peppy Grill was a late-night greasy spoon diner in Indianapolis's Fountain Square neighborhood. Herron art students, hipsters, Appalachian transplants, and others often congregated there after late nights out at the bars. It was originally part of a chain that started at Washington Street and Senate Avenue in Indianapolis. It grew to 10 locations by 1960. It served eggs, bacon, and other fare 24/7, with many filing in after the bars closed at 2 a.m. on weekends. It closed in 2019 for an extensive renovation into a more modern, stylized version of a traditional American diner with "hamburgs" that regulars decried as a faux replica and theme park version. It reopened at the worst possible time during the pandemic and served its last cup of joe in 2021.

FAST FOOD

Indiana loves its fast food. Fast-food restaurants flank nearly every highway exit. There are even suburban-style White Castle and Arby's restaurants with drive-throughs smack-dab in downtown Indianapolis. The city is home to the headquarters of Steak 'n Shake, the 1950s-style steakburger diner the film critic Roger Ebert ranked as one of his favorite restaurants and that is also beloved for its chili. Schoop's in Northwest Indiana often ranks as one of the best burger joints in the country. Papa John's got its start in Jeffersonville. McDonald's by far has the most fast-food restaurants in Indiana, which ranked sixth nationwide in one study with 46 fast-food restaurants for every 100,000 residents. Indiana birthed the popular Burger Chef chain and other fast-food joints that now live on only in nostalgic memory.

Courtesy of the Library of Congress

Burger Chef

Indiana's own Burger Chef was the Burger King of yesteryear. Brothers Frank and Donald Thomas invented a flame broiler and opened the first Burger Chef in Indianapolis in 1957. It grew into a national restaurant chain by locating in small towns and reached more than 1,200 locations by 1972, becoming the second-biggest burger chain nationally after only McDonald's. It was known for its Big Shef double burger, quarter-pound Super Shef, and works bar where customers added their own toppings. It had a mascot called Burger Chef, his sidekick Jeff, and friends like Count Fangburger and Burgerini, whose adventures were recounted in its Funmeal, the first kids' meal, which predated McDonald's Happy Meal. The chain was eventually sold to Hardee's, which converted most of its restaurants to Hardee's and occasionally brings back the Big Shef. The last Burger Chef closed in 1996.

Courtesy of John Margolies

A&W Root Beer Barrel

A&W is known throughout the Midwest for its frosty root beer, hot dogs, and cheese curds. The Wisconsin-based restaurant used to operate out of root beer barrels. The A&W Root Beer Barrels were landmarks at the southeast corner of US 31 and Ireland Road and on Western Avenue in South Bend. The Western Avenue location later became home to the since-shuttered Chauncey's Restaurant. A&W's footprint across Indiana has shrunk considerably, but the chain still has locations in Indianapolis, Muncie, Greensburg, Marion, and Richmond, none of which are operated out of anything as distinctive as a root beer barrel. Culver's, the popular purveyor of butter burgers, cheese curds, and all things Wisconsin, has emerged as something of a spiritual successor.

Courtesy of Elkhart County Historical Society

BOOGIE BURGER

Boogie Burger never aspired to be more than a neighborhood burger and malt shop. But the hippie-inspired burger joint built up a cult following during its decade in Indianapolis's hipster Broad Ripple neighborhood. The chill burger restaurant, which lined the walls with art in a space *Indianapolis Monthly* likened to a broom closet, grilled up a variety of creative burgers with toppings like peanut butter, fried eggs, and pastrami. Its most popular burger was the Wild West, which took the western burger up a notch with beer-battered onion rings. It had a cult following for its banana pudding shakes and garlic fries that some said were so garlicky they would burn your mouth. It closed in 2017 after its owners decided to retire.

The Lure

The Lure was a 1950s-style drive-in that fed generations in Northwest Indiana. The family-owned restaurant first opened on West Fifth Avenue in downtown Gary and expanded to Merrillville and Portage. It claimed its hamburgers, roast beef, ham and cheese, and fish filet sandwiches were "always the best." It sliced its medium rare roast beef right on the spot and served it in a sesame seed bun. It also catered to sweet tooths with its shakes and slices of apple pie. Nicky's Gyros operates out of the Portage location on Melton Road. The vintage Lure sign was still up by the roadside until high winds knocked it down in 2023, but the intact old-school signage on the building still makes it look like a Lure restaurant from the street.

LOCAL PRODUCTS

Indiana feeds the nation. It's of course best known for commodity crops like corn and soybeans, but it also produces food products like Albanese Gummi Bears, Red Gold ketchup, and Tortillas Nuevo Leon's flour tortillas. The American Licorice Company makes black licorice in LaPorte. Meats by Linz in Hammond supplies high-end steak houses across the country. El Popular in East Chicago sells chorizo, mole, and chocolate from coast to coast. The popcorn king Orville Redenbacher used to be based in Valparaiso. But as conglomerates have bought up smaller companies or crowded competitors off store shelves, not all the locally manufactured food products in Indiana have survived.

Peerless Potato Chips

Peerless Potato Chips started in Gary in 1928 just before the Great Depression. World War I Royal Flying Corps pilot John Norman Hogg was dispatched from Britain to Canada to train pilots, began working in the steel business in Sault Ste. Marie, and ended up chasing opportunity in the booming mill town of Gary. He made the greasy, salty Peerless chips that were widely distributed around Northwest Indiana for nearly 90 years. Region natives returning home stocked up on the local favorites, which were made with potatoes from Indiana, Florida, and North Dakota, depending on the season. His oldest son, Jack Hogg, took over the business, but it closed when he became terminally ill. It had been in decline for years due to a decline in shelf space for local products. A new owner tried to revive it but had trouble getting the old-school machinery working again.

Courtesy of Historic American Buldings Survey

ROSELYN BAKERY

Roselyn Bakery's instantly recognized flying V-shaped signs were a landmark across Indiana. John and Mildred Clark opened the first bakery on North Meridian Street in 1943. It served up signature items like Sweetheart Coffee Cake, Blackout Cake, and Zebra Square Brownies. It grew to about 40 locations across Central Indiana. However, the chain dissolved after the Indiana State Department of Health shut down the central baking facility in 1999. The owners founded Roselyn Recipe the next year to continue to make baked goods for grocery stores. Kroger supermarkets in the Indianapolis area still carry some of its baked goods, including its Hot Cross Buns and Alligator Coffee Cake.

PLUTO WATER

When nature won't, Pluto will, the tagline went. Named after the Roman god of the underworld since it was sourced from underground reservoirs, the mineral water was bottled from natural mineral springs in French Lick. Billed as "America's laxative," it was sold at the West Baden Springs Hotel and around the country in bottles. It took 450 railroad cars to ship it to market in 1919. Sodium, magnesium, and other natural laxatives made it effective in about half an hour to two hours. It also was seen as a cure for other ailments. Louis Armstrong's mother for instance gave it to him for lockjaw. Production stopped in 1971 when lithium was deemed a controlled substance because the water contained lithium salts.

Courtesy of Geoffrey A. Landis via Wikimedia Commons

El Frio

El Frio was one of the largest Black-owned pop manufacturers in the United States. The business on 19th Avenue in Gary made 10 different flavors, like orange soda, Afro Cola, and lemon-lime soda, and it landed local franchises to produce Joe Louis Punch and Cadillac Sodas. It was founded in 1946 by William Henry Coleman, a Mississippi native who studied at Froebel High School in Gary, Gary College, and the Indiana University–Gary Center before going to Roosevelt University in Chicago. An avid reader and Sunday school superintendent, Coleman launched several business ventures, including a scavenger service. El Frio expanded and moved to a larger location at 2225 Broadway in Gary when white stores started stocking the products during segregation. The company dissolved in the 1970s when Coleman left the private sector to serve under Richard Hatcher, one of the country's first Black mayors. He served in several roles, including city controller.

Polk's Best Jersey Milk Depot

Polk's Best Jersey Milk was a nationally recognized dairy based in Greenwood. James T. Polk, who also ran the largest cannery west of Baltimore in Greenwood, founded Polk's Best Jersey Milk Depot at 325 East Seventh Street in Greenwood in 1893 with the slogan "cleanliness is next to godliness," keeping its stalls immaculate. Polk focused heavily on quality, installing the best machinery available to process the milk, taking good care of the dairy cows, and shielding them from the weather. The Polks also canned vegetables on their stove, which they sold worldwide under the brand Polk's Best.

Courtesy of Indiana Historical Society

Parrott-Taggart Crackers

Burton Parrott, a descendant of the sea captain John Parrott, and Alexander Taggart started the Parrott-Taggart Baking Company in Indianapolis in 1885. Five years later, Taggart started the United States Baking Company, which merged into the National Biscuit Company and eventually became Nabisco. The Parrott-Taggart Baking Company plant served as its local factory and a producer of Parrott-Taggart brand crackers, which were sold with a label that featured a moon with a human face eating a cracker. The industrial bakery employed 150 people and ran through 30,000 barrels of flour a month. It also made snaps, biscuits, and bread.

Courtesy of the Library of Congress

{ENTERTAINMENT}

The fertile soil of Indiana has produced many legendary entertainers, like David Letterman, Axl Rose, Jenna Fischer, Florence Henderson, Red Skelton, Mike Epps, Vivica A. Fox, Betsy Palmer, Anne Baxter, Karl Malden, Fred "The Hammer" Williamson, Best Actor Oscar winner Brendan Fraser, and Garfield creator Jim Davis, who reminds us that lasagna is good but Mondays not so much. The Hoosier State was once home to many magnificent vaudeville stages, opulent opera halls, and grand movie palaces that no longer line the landscape. The State Theatre in Hammond was blown up with a satchel full of dynamite in what was likely insurance fraud, but that was probably the most dramatic case. More venues suffered slow declines and eventual demolitions due to changing tastes and times, getting replaced by the multiplexes that themselves have become endangered in the streaming era. Indiana has also lost sports stadiums, amusement parks, and many other attractions where people had fun and made fond memories. Drive-in movie theaters, for instance, have largely fallen out of fashion despite Joe Bob Briggs's declaration that the drive-in will never die. Few amusement parks remain, let alone ones that display bears, tigers, or other wild animals. The past sometimes has a perception of being staid, but, historically, entertainment in the Hoosier State used to be a little wilder than a night of Netflix and DoorDash.

Balloon spectacle
Courtesy of Johnson's Indy 500

John Dillinger's fake wooden gun

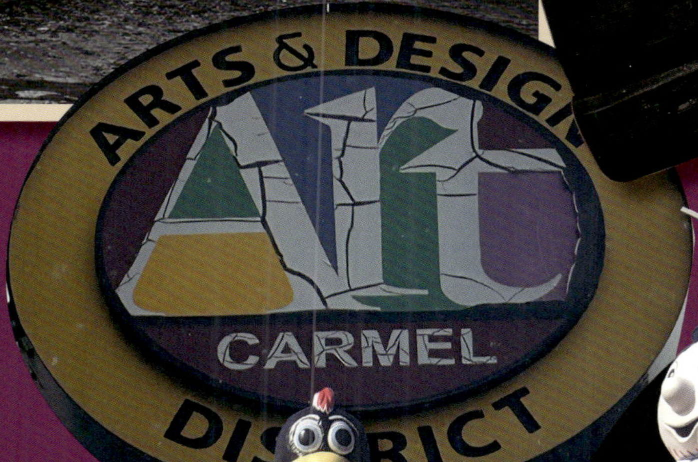

Sauzer's Kiddieland
Courtesy of *The Times of Northwest Indiana*

Courtesy of Calumet Regional Archives

Mascot Hall of Fame

AMUSEMENT PARKS

Indiana remains home to a few amusement parks, like Holiday World and Splashin' Safari in Santa Claus and Indiana Beach Amusement and Water Park in Monticello, the "riviera of the Midwest" that incessantly bombarded eardrums with the jingle "There's more than corn in Indiana." People still flock there to ride wooden roller coasters, take boat tours of Lake Shafer, and play carnival games. But thrills along the boardwalk were once far more common at amusement parks, which were once far more prevalent in Indiana than now. The bright lights of the midways once crammed with penny arcades, carousels, and other rides have dimmed.

Courtesy of the *Times of Northwest Indiana*

Riverside

Courtesy of Boston Public Library

In the early 20th century, Indianapolis was home to several amusement parks, like the White City Amusement Park in Broad Ripple and Wonderland Amusement Park on the east side. Riverside Amusement Park had a run of 67 years by Riverside City Park on West 30th Street between White River and the Central Canal. It launched in 1903 with eight roller coasters, a mirror maze, and other attractions. It was free to get into the park, but it cost a fee to go on rides like the Old Mill Ride in which people took a boat through a replica flour mill. About 30,000 people, roughly one-third of Indy's population at the time, showed up on opening day in 1906. It kept adding new attractions, like a dancing pavilion, roller-skating, Dodgem cars, and a beach with a six-story diving tower. But it shuttered in 1970.

Enchanted Forest

Enchanted Forest in Porter was billed as "the playground of the Indiana Dunes." The amusement park was situated at the busy intersection of US 20 and Indiana 49 near the entrance to the Indiana Dunes State Park. With enough parking for 1,500 cars, it featured rides like the Mad Mouse Roller Coaster, the Skyliner, the Tilt-a-Whirl, the Octopus, and the Scrambler. It had a Ferris wheel, tram, and kiddie boat, as well as go-karts that cost extra to race around. The Enchanted Forest had many groves where visitors could picnic. It welcomed large groups, including from schools, churches, and nearby steel mills in Northwest Indiana. It ran from 1957 to 1991, when it became Splash Down Dunes Water Park and then the Seven Peaks Water Park Duneland. The most recent incarnation closed for good in 2017.

Courtesy of *The Times of Northwest Indiana*

Courtesy of the *Times of Northwest Indiana*

Sauzer's Kiddieland

Generations of kids made memories at Sauzer's Kiddieland, a popular amusement park at the Crossroads of the Nation intersection of US 30 and US 41 in Schererville. The Sauzer family operated the 15-acre park at one of Northwest Indiana's busiest intersections from 1949 to 1993. A regional attraction, it had a paddleboat pond, the Sauzer's Waffle House Restaurant, and 18 rides, including coasters, a swan ride, a sky fighter, bumper cars, a Tilt-a-Whirl, and a Ferris wheel. Kids could ride on ponies or the miniature train. The Swingin' Gyms live on at the Amusement Preservation Museum in Grafton, Ohio.

Wonderland
Amusement Park

Courtesy of Wikimedia Commons

Wonderland Amusement Park was a short-lived trolley park around a lake near Irvington. Costing a dime to enter, the Coney Island–esque park featured a scenic railway ride, a dance pavilion, a 125-foot electric tower, and cigarette-smoking bears. It was located on Indianapolis's east side, where it opened in 1906. Vaudevillians, acrobats, aerialists, and animal acts performed on the sprawling 24-building campus that was illuminated with 50,000 light bulbs and raked by a 100,000-watt searchlight. Inspired by the White City of the 1893 Chicago World's Fair, it had an arch engraved with "Wonderland" at the entrance, a funhouse, an arcade, a ride simulating the Johnstown Flood, and a dirigible that went up for flights twice daily. It added new attractions every year, including the trained bull Big Bill, stunt bicyclists, lions, and an unlicensed "blind tiger" beer garden that was raided by police. It burned down in 1911.

Rose Island

Courtesy of Jefferson Township Public Library

The Rose Island Amusement Park had a 14-year run near Charlestown on the Devil's Backbone peninsula where the Fourteen Mile Creek flowed into the Ohio River in Southern Indiana. It was previously a church camp known as Fern Grove. The Louisville and Jefferson Ferry Company bought it to boost its ferry business, bringing in church picnics, family outings, and other social gatherings. David Rose bought it in 1923 and built a 118-acre amusement park with a wooden roller coaster, Ferris wheel, rolling-skating rink, dance hall, swimming pool, and hotel. A zoo included monkeys, wolves, and a black bear nicknamed Teddy Roosevelt. It was accessible by steamboat, including what would become the *Belle of Louisville*. It closed because of a 1937 flood that submerged the park under 10 feet of water. The abandoned amusement park lies in what's now the Charlestown State Park.

SPORTS VENUES

Indiana is known as a hotbed for sports. Notre Dame football is a national brand that's been long broadcast on NBC. Indiana University basketball has rafters filled with championship banners. Peyton Manning brought home a title to Indianapolis and is why there's a generation of kids named Peyton. Indy is a major sports city, hosting Final Fours, Big Ten Championships, and even a Super Bowl. The Indianapolis 500 is billed as the largest single-day sporting event in the world. The Hoosier State spawned classic sports films like *Hoosiers, Rudy*, and *Breaking Away*. *A League of Their Own* was filmed at Evansville's Bosse Field. But some of the state's most thrilling sports moments took place in venues that are no longer with us today.

Courtesy of Wikimedia Commons

Market Square Arena

Elvis played his final concert at Market Square Arena in Indianapolis in 1977. The nearly 17,000-seat venue opened on an entire city block of Market Street in downtown Indy in 1974, serving as home to the Pacers, Racers, Checkers, Ice, and Twisters. It had a monochrome scoreboard like in Detroit's Joe Louis Arena and hosted the 1985 NBA All-Star Game as well as many concerts. It was mainly known as the home of the city's American Basketball Association and then National Basketball Association teams until it was shuttered in 1999 to be replaced by what's now the Gainbridge Fieldhouse. It was demolished in 2001, when it was imploded in only 12 seconds. A memorial to Elvis marks the site where it once stood.

Courtesy of IMCPL

Hoosier Dome

Courtesy of IMCPL

The Hoosier Dome in Indianapolis wasn't paid off until 2020, 13 years after it was demolished. The astroturf football stadium was built in 1984 in the style of Minneapolis's Hubert H. Humphrey Metrodome and Detroit's Pontiac Silverdome with the goal of luring a National Football League franchise to the Circle City. The Baltimore Colts packed up Mayflower trucks and headed to Indy in the dead of night. The stadium sat only about 56,000 for football, making it the smallest in the NFL. It hosted its largest-ever crowd for WrestleMania in 1992 and was renamed the RCA Dome in 1994. The dome was deflated and the stadium demolished in 2008. People for Urban Progress salvaged the fabric roof and turned it into bags, wallets, purses, and art pieces it has sold around town.

MARION INTERNATIONAL MOTORCYCLE RACE

The Marion International Motorcycle Championship Race, known as the Cornfield Classic, took place on a five-mile course on back roads southwest of town. It was billed as "the greatest event of its kind" when it launched in 1919. Harley-Davidson sent a team known as the Wrecking Crew and swept the top three places in the first year, with Red Parkhurst winning and Otto Walker clearing 100 mph. It beat rivals Indian and Excelsior, establishing Harley-Davidson as the leading motorcycle manufacturer. More than 15,000 people turned out to the 1920 race, which ran for 200 miles and three hours. Harley-Davidson rider Ray Weishaar won. He was handed a piglet from a local farm, which he took as a passenger on a victory lap. That led to Harley-Davidson's race team becoming known as the Hog Boys, Marion getting called the Home of the Hog, and the Hog nickname becoming synonymous with the motorcycle.

Jungle Park Speedway

The Jungle Park Speedway was a proving ground for the Indianapolis 500, producing eight winners, including the four-time victor Wilbur Shaw. The half-mile oval in Bloomingdale was a premier speedway in the early 20th century but shuttered in 1960 after a series of deadly accidents. It was built in 1925 when auto racing was fledgling. Six people died in the first few years, including an official repairing a divot on the track, a spectator, and drivers, including one whose skull was crushed when he was thrown into a tree. The track lacked an outside retainer wall, so cars that whipped around high-banked turns at more than 100 mph often went flying into trees and Sugar Creek. Spectators put out fires with their beer bottles. Racing ended for good after a car flew into the stands, killing a 37-year-old Terre Haute woman. Wooden grandstands and a few other remnants remain today.

Curt DeBaun via Flickr

Wigwam

The Wigwam Sports Complex in Anderson was the second-largest high school gym in a state famously crazed about high school basketball. The 8,996-seat gym opened in 1961 and was technically called the Anderson High School Athletic and Educational Building. It was always known as the Wigwam due to the team's Indians nickname and its huge mural of an Indian chief. It opened as a basketball gym with a pool, cafeteria, stage, and vocational training classrooms. It was expanded with academic and auditorium wings in 1979. Architect Arthur B. Henning designed it with large exterior self-supporting steel beams and columns that ensured the views were unobstructed by interior beams. Listed on the National Register of Historic Places, the venue hosted Ray Charles, Robert F. Kennedy, Richard Nixon, Hillary Clinton, and the Indiana Pacers, including when they played in the ABA Eastern Conference Finals in 1969. The school board closed the Wigwam in 2011, but plans to renovate and adaptively reuse the landmark have since been broached.

Courtesy of Madison County Historian

Owen J. Bush Stadium

The Owen J. Bush baseball stadium hosted the Indianapolis Indians minor-league team from 1931 to 1996, when Victory Field was built downtown. It previously hosted Negro League teams like the Indianapolis Clowns and the Indianapolis Capitols, the final champion in the Continental Football League. Indians owner Norm Perry built it and named it Perry Stadium to honor his brother Jim, the team's previous owner who was killed in a plane crash. Osborn Engineering, which also built Yankee Stadium, designed the ballpark. English ivy was painted on its brick outfield walls, which inspired P. K. Wrigley to plant ivy in the Cubs stadium. It was later named Victory Field during World War II and then Bush Stadium after former player and Indians president Owen J. "Donie" Bush.

16th Street Speedway

Owen J. Bush Stadium was turned into a midget car racetrack called the 16th Street Speedway after the Indianapolis Indians moved to White River State Park in the 1990s. The track proved short-lived. But the historic ballpark had many uses over the years. *Eight Men Out* was filmed there in 1987, when it also hosted the baseball tournament in the Pan Am Games. It was used for car storage during the Cash for Clunkers program and later turned into the Stadium Lofts apartment complex, which retained part of the historic architecture like the lights, exterior facade, ticket booth, and owner's suite.

Courtesy of Wikimedia Commons

Indianapolis Tennis Center

The Indianapolis Tennis Center hosted professional, amateur, and collegiate tennis at the Indiana University–Purdue University at Indianapolis campus by the White River. The complex with both indoor and outdoor courts was known as the Indianapolis Sports Center when it opened in 1979. It seated 10,000 and hosted the US Men's Clay Court Championships and the 1987 Pan Am Games. It also doubled as a music venue in the 1980s, hosting big name acts like Elton John, Billy Idol, the Grateful Dead, Tom Petty, Donna Summer, and Jimmy Buffett. Offering sweeping views of the downtown skyline, it also hosted the Indy Jazz Fest and one of the city's first LGBT Pride events. It lost the RCA Tennis Championships in 2007 and was torn down three years later.

James Keesling via Flickr

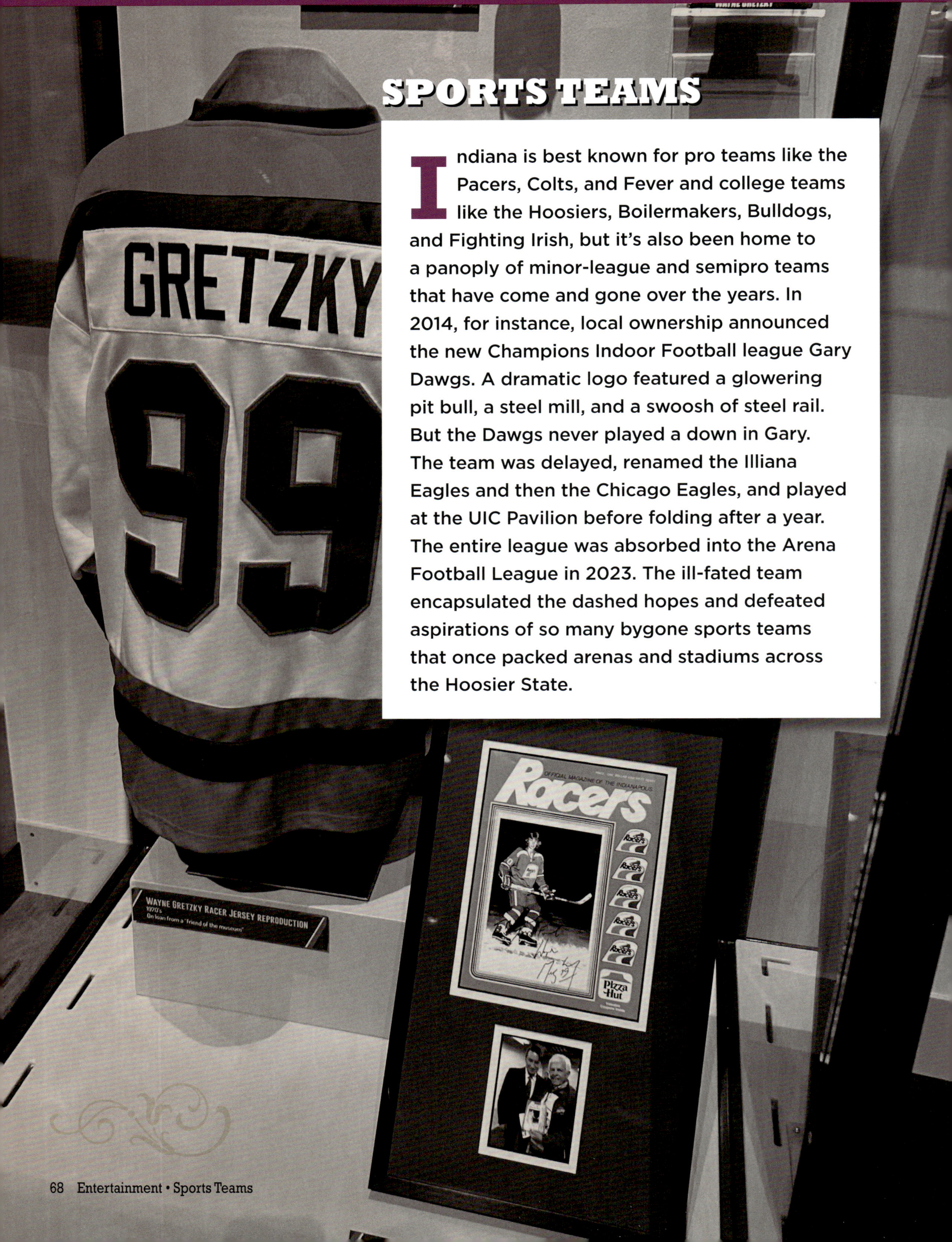

SPORTS TEAMS

Indiana is best known for pro teams like the Pacers, Colts, and Fever and college teams like the Hoosiers, Boilermakers, Bulldogs, and Fighting Irish, but it's also been home to a panoply of minor-league and semipro teams that have come and gone over the years. In 2014, for instance, local ownership announced the new Champions Indoor Football league Gary Dawgs. A dramatic logo featured a glowering pit bull, a steel mill, and a swoosh of steel rail. But the Dawgs never played a down in Gary. The team was delayed, renamed the Illiana Eagles and then the Chicago Eagles, and played at the UIC Pavilion before folding after a year. The entire league was absorbed into the Arena Football League in 2023. The ill-fated team encapsulated the dashed hopes and defeated aspirations of so many bygone sports teams that once packed arenas and stadiums across the Hoosier State.

Indianapolis Racers

The 1970s were a wild time for upstart professional sports leagues. The NBA faced a challenge from the ABA, while the World Hockey Association took on the National Hockey League. The WHA's Indianapolis Racers played in Market Square Arena downtown from 1974 to 1978, taking on rivals like the Cincinnati Stingers and the Cleveland Crusaders. The team had the league's leading attendance one season and had an incredible pedigree—it was the first pro team the immortal Hall of Famers Wayne Gretzky and Mark Messier played for. But unlike the Pacers, which jumped from the ABA to the NBA, the Racers didn't join the Edmonton Oilers, Winnipeg Jets, Hartford Whalers, and Quebec Nordiques in making the jump when the WHA folded; NHL officials feared Indy was too small a market to support a team. The city is now home to the Indy Fuel, a minor-league affiliate of the Chicago Blackhawks.

Courtesy of Tom Hagerty via Wikimedia Commons

Fort Wayne Mad Ants

Indiana's second-largest city has a rich history of minor-league sports, including the Fort Wayne TinCaps baseball team and the Fort Wayne Komets hockey team. The NBA G League Fort Wayne Mad Ants played at the Allen County War Memorial Coliseum from 2007 to 2023 before relocating to Noblesville, closer to the team's Indiana Pacers affiliate. Part of the NBA Development League, or D-League, it won a championship in the 2013–14 season. It was named after the city namesake, Revolutionary War general Mad Anthony Wayne. The Mad Ants filled a void after the Continental Basketball Association's Fort Wayne Fury folded in 1991. Over the years, it was affiliated with the Milwaukee Bucks, Charlotte Hornets, and Detroit Pistons until it was acquired by the Pacers in 2015. NBA players like Khris Middleton, Miles Plumlee, Jordan Crawford, and Noah Vonleh took the court for the Mad Ants over the years.

Fort Wayne Pistons

The Los Angeles Lakers are one of the most storied franchises in all of sports. Few people realize they started out as the Detroit Gems in 1946. Detroit was home to several early professional basketball teams, including the Eagles, Falcons, and Vagabond Kings. The Detroit Pistons that earned a "Bad Boys" moniker in the 1980s actually called Indiana home for the first two decades of their existence. The Zollner Corporation, a foundry that made pistons for car engines, sponsored the Fort Wayne Pistons, originally a semipro team that joined the NBA predecessor National Basketball League, winning the championship in 1944 and 1945. The team was accused of throwing the 1955 NBA Finals to the Syracuse Nationals and of shaving points for gamblers. In 1957, the owner decided Fort Wayne was too small a market and moved the team to the Motor City, then the fifth-largest city in the country.

Courtesy of the Allen County Public Library

Gary Bears

The Chicago Bears had fans throughout Indiana until the Colts moved from Baltimore to Indianapolis. They remain popular in Northwest Indiana, just outside the city, and nearly ended up in Gary. In the 1990s, the McCaskeys were looking to move away from the aging Soldier Field, the smallest stadium in the league. Northwest Indiana officials mounted a full-court press to try to build a new Bears stadium on the Lake Michigan lakefront in Gary, similar to how both the New York Giants and Jets play in New Jersey. They pitched an entertainment complex around the stadium called Planet Park that would have included bars, restaurants, retail, hotels, and a nine-hole golf course—similar to the proposed Michael Jackson Museum that also never materialized. Mayor Richard Daley vehemently opposed the move, threatening to sue the Bears so they could no longer use Chicago in their name if they moved outside city limits. Along with balloon rides over Lake Michigan and the Michael Jackson Museum, Planet Park was one of the many pie-in-the-sky Gary redevelopment proposals that ended up lost to history, but bids to lure away the Bears continued with state lawmakers establishing a Northwest Indiana sports committee in 2025.

Indianapolis Clowns

Courtesy of IMCPL

Indianapolis was home to several Negro League teams like the ABCs, American Giants, Athletics, and Crawfords, but the best known was perhaps the Clowns, who have been compared to the Harlem Globetrotters. Greats like Goose Tatum and Choo-Choo Coleman played for the team, which was known for comedic showmanship. It did barnstorming tours that included stunts like pantomimed shadow ball without an actual ball, oversized gloves, and pitching balls between their legs or behind their backs. The antics inspired the movie *The Bingo Long Traveling All-Stars & Motor Kings* starring Richard Pryor, James Earl Jones, and Billy Dee Williams. The team started in Miami, moved to Cincinnati, and then relocated to Indianapolis, where it won the league title three times in the 1950s. Home run king Hank Aaron signed for the team for $200 a month in 1953, batting cleanup until his contract was sold for $10,000 to the Boston Braves. The team signed second baseman Toni Stone as the first woman to play competitively with a long-term contract. The Clowns barnstormed until the 1960s.

Courtesy of *The Times of Northwest Indiana*

Gary Steelheads

The Genesis Convention Center was built in downtown Gary in the hope of sparking a renaissance. For a decade, the now-idled convention center hosted the Gary Steelheads, a professional team that won the 2006 Continental Basketball Association Eastern Conference championship. The Steelheads played in the CBA, International Basketball League, and Continental Basketball Association. Indiana University standout Dane Fife, who was a starter on the 2002 IU squad that made it to the Final Four, laced up for the Steelheads in his only professional season of basketball. Oliver "Big O" Miller, a former Phoenix Suns center who was infamous for being the heaviest player in NBA history at 380 pounds, also played for the Steelheads. The team's owner, Jewell Harris Sr., was indicted on federal extortion charges in 2006, and the team eventually folded.

Hammond Pros

Hammond was home to one of the original teams that made up the American Professional Football Association, the National Football League's predecessor. The Hammond Pros rarely played in Hammond, instead mostly playing road games against teams like the Detroit Heralds and the Canton Bulldogs. The team played home games at Cubs Park in neighboring Chicago. The Pros lasted only from 1917 to 1926, but the team fielded three future Hall of Famers. Paddy Driscoll was the NFL's first All Pro quarterback and leading scorer for two years. Fritz Pollard was the league's first Black coach. George Halas played wide receiver for the Pros before founding the Chicago Bears and becoming the namesake of the NFC Championship trophy. The Pros failed to make the cut when the NFL trimmed down to 12 teams in 1926, departing most of the small Midwestern markets where it got its start.

Courtesy of the Hammond Public Library

FILM

I once saw the documentary *The King of Kong: A Fistful of Quarters* at Key Cinema, a bygone art-house theater near the University of Indianapolis campus on Indy's south side. We were the only people to show up to the movie, enjoying what felt like a private screening in an otherwise empty theater. Cinematic magic has faded at many movie theaters across the state. But Indiana still has a rich film history. It gave the world silver-screen icons James Dean and Steve McQueen and acclaimed screenwriters Steve Tesich and Angelo Pizzo. Many movies have been filmed in the Hoosier State, like *Public Enemies, Pearl Harbor, Prancer, Natural Born Killers, Hard Rain, Columbus,* and the Casey Affleck vehicle *Lonesome Jim*, which was shot almost entirely in Goshen.

Courtesy of Freepik

Courtesy of the Gary Public Library

The Palace Theater

The Palace Theater in downtown Gary is today best known as a symbol of blight that's sought out by urban explorers and photographers looking to splash crumbling, decrepit buildings that look bombed out all over Instagram. The Steel City was featured on the television series *Life After People* to show what a postapocalyptic future would look like. The long-abandoned movie palace at 791 Broadway was designed by the prolific architect John Eberson, who earned the nickname "Opera House John" after designing more than 500 movie palaces, including in Paris and Australia. He also designed the surviving Paramount Theatre in Anderson in his signature atmospheric style that gave the impression of an open-air starry sky overhead. The Palace was a grand venue that hosted movies, vaudeville acts, and live stage shows. It shut down in 1972 when Gary's steel industry was declining. A few restoration plans went nowhere.

Plan 9 Film Emporium

In its waning years, Plan 9 Film Emporium in Bloomington had a sarcastic handwritten note by the counter saying, "VHS is totally due for a comeback." The countercultural video store recognized the writing was on the wall as streaming came to succeed it. In its heyday, it was a glorious repository of indie, art-house, foreign, cult, and otherwise obscure films. It's where IU students and faculty flocked to find movies by directors like Steven Soderbergh, Wim Wenders, and Jim Jarmusch. It's where I expanded my cinematic horizons by stumbling on classics I had never heard of, like *Withnail and I.* The selection was immense and well curated by a staff of passionate cinephiles.

Von Lee

Bloomington's Von Lee Theater screened movies for decades. The venerable movie theater on Kirkwood Avenue just past the Sample Gates of the Indiana University campus served as an art-house theater, showing many indie, intellectual, and foreign films over the years. It's where IU students flocked for cinematic edification and education. It eventually shuttered and was transformed into a Noodles and Co., though the building's distinct architectural facade was maintained. IU Bloomington helped fill the void by opening the Indiana University Cinema, a repurposing of the historic IU Theatre that staged plays. Four panels of Thomas Hart Benton's *Indiana Murals* adorn the new movie palace that opened in 2011.

Courtesy of IU

Courtesy of the *Indiana Daily Student*

The Cinemat

Former Bloomington City Councilman Steve Volan owned the hipster movie rental spot the Cinemat, which was like if an art-house theater and Blockbuster had a baby. Similar to renowned video stores like Seattle's Scarecrow Video, it specialized in indie, foreign, documentary, experimental, LGBT, and other genres of filmmaking underrepresented in mainstream culture. Founded in 2002, the video store at 123 South Walnut Street had a screening room with lawn chairs and craft beers where people could watch screenings or cultural events like the weekly Anything After 10 comedy show. Dr. Calamari and Baron Mardi also hosted the weekly Atomic Age Cinema screenings on Saturdays at midnight to roast cheesy horror films. The cinephile's paradise ended up closing in 2009, selling its inventory to the similar but longer-running Plan 9 Video.

The Tivoli Theatre

The Tivoli Theatre screened its first film in Michigan City in 1922 and would have a run time of a half century. Architect Henry L. Newhouse designed the neoclassical movie theater with a white terra-cotta facade. The $300,000 theater went up at the site of the Grand Opera House, which had burned down the previous year. The 1,300-seat theater originally hosted vaudeville, stage shows, and movies. It had a stage and orchestra pit. The Balaban & Katz chain acquired the Tivoli in the 1930s, and it hosted the Miss Indiana Pageant from 1957 to 1961. Kerasotes ran the Tivoli until it closed in 1972 with a screening of the horror movie *The Rats Are Coming! The Werewolves Are Here!*

Courtesy of Michigan City Historical Society

Ski-Hi Drive-In

The Ski-Hi was one of the grandest drive-ins in Muncie. The Auto Park Theater was the first to open in Muncie in 1946, followed by the larger Muncie Drive-In the following year. The Ski-Hi opened on a 20-acre site just north of town at the heavily trafficked intersection of State Roads 3 and 28 in 1950. It boasted amenities like moonglow lighting, In-a-Car speakers, and a "mammoth clear-vision screen." It cost $100,000 to construct and had a 64-foot-tall screen, which was one of the biggest in the Hoosier State. It remained a popular destination for moviegoers for years but finally closed in 2005 after years of decline as more people headed to the multiplexes.

Courtesy of Ball State University

Town Theatre

Courtesy of Calumet Regional Archives

Someone once joked that watching *A Christmas Story*, which Jean Shepherd wrote about his Hammond childhood, at the Town Theatre in downtown Highland was the most Region experience one could have. The single-screen theater on Kennedy Avenue showed many independent films, including the Miramax movies in the 1990s. It screened films like Todd Solondz's *Welcome to the Dollhouse*, *Brassed Off*, and *My Big Fat Greek Wedding*, which ran for months due to its popularity among Northwest Indiana's large Greek community. Known for its eccentricities, it was decorated with knight armor and the Greek masks of comedy and tragedy. It had an intermission in which the red velvet drapes closed halfway through the film, and everyone filed out to the lobby for cake, coffee, and conversation. It closed when the owners died. The town acquired it and had plans to turn it into a performing arts venue but ended up demolishing it.

Rivoli Theatre

Courtesy of Delaware County Historical Society

The Rivoli Theatre was one of downtown Muncie's many movie theaters from Hollywood's Golden Age, including the Orpheum, Uptown, Star, Strand, Theatorium, Majestic, Lyric, Crystal, Columbia, and Wysor Grand. The Rivoli was built by Chicago's Fitzpatrick-McElroy Company, which the *Muncie Evening Press* said "spent a small fortune on the lavish furnishings alone." Described as "a bit of old Spain," the 2,000-seat theater was palatial with velvet carpets, rich tapestries, Spanish mirrors, wrought-iron lamps, arches hung with silken draperies, and a glaring 10,000-watt marquee. It hosted vaudeville acts on weekends and had a Wurlitzer Style E organ that accompanied silent films. It opened in 1927 with five vaudeville acts and a screening of *The Perfect Sap*. It had premieres with searchlights, flowers, radio broadcasts, and crowds dressed to the nines. It closed after screening *An American Tail* and *The Morning After* as its final films in 1987.

Y & W DRIVE-IN
in Merrillville

The Y & W Drive-In in Merrillville opened in 1953 with screenings of Disney and Bugs Bunny cartoons and would go on to delight moviegoers for decades. The drive-in stood on the main drag of Broadway with a neon sign that could be seen blocks away. One could even see the movies while driving by. It was home to as many as three screens, including one that could fit 940 cars. It had amenities like a playground, the bingo-like game of Banko, and a small zoo with monkeys. It hosted fireworks on holidays and would show movies from dusk to dawn on New Year's Eve, ringing in the New Year with doughnuts and coffee. It had double features and triple features in the 1980s. It closed in 1997 after years of decline. It was demolished in 2004.

Courtesy of Ross Township Historical Society

Indiana Theater

The Indiana Theater in Terre Haute still stands but has long been used as an events venue that no longer screens films. The theater opened in 1922 as John Eberson's first atmospheric design with a ceiling evoking a starlit sky. He sought to create a dream theater that was inspired by the Spanish Andalusia and featured ceilings with Moorish designs, 38 statues, a Roman amphitheater-like auditorium, and an intercom system to help ushers find open seats. It wowed with a 3,000-light peacock marquee and one of the largest screens in the state. The 2,018-seat Indiana Theater opened to much fanfare with live peacocks, a 30-piece orchestra, and a fashion show from Siegel's Department Store. It hosted a number of noted entertainers, such as Frank Sinatra, the Marx Brothers, and Red Skelton. The Vigo County Capital Improvement Board has been considering turning it over to the private sector.

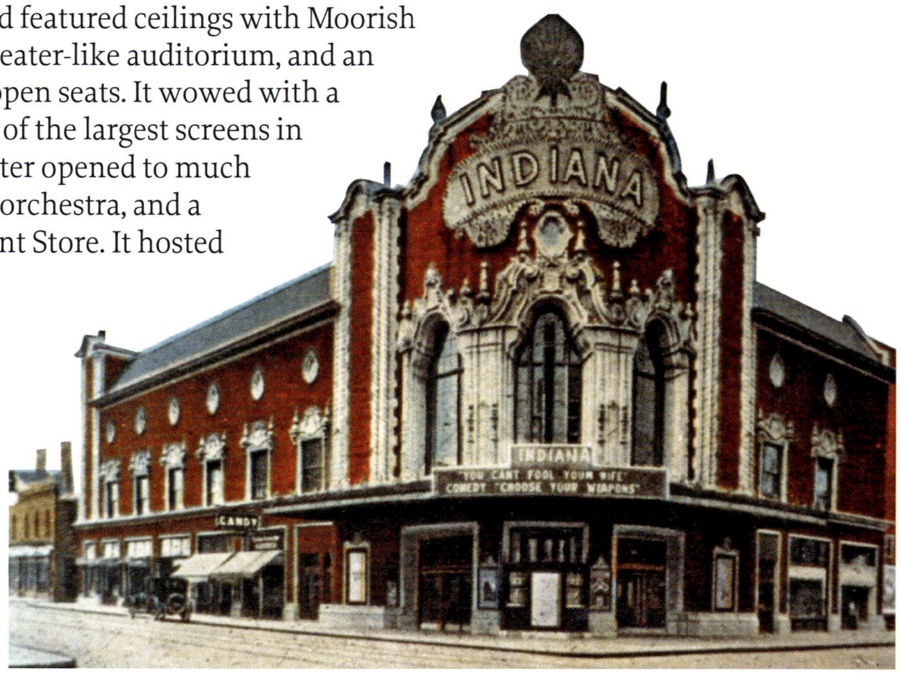

Courtesy of Vigo County History Center

Premier Theater

Originally known as the Shauers Theater, the Premier Theater brought Hollywood films to downtown Valparaiso for more than 60 years. The movie palace at Lincolnway and Lafayette Street opened in 1921 and ran until a six-screen multiplex opened up at an outdoor mall in the early 1980s. Gustav George Shauer founded the theater after buying an orchard near Flint Lake in Valparaiso in the early 1900s. It screened free cartoons, drew long lines when big movies came out, and served hometown magnate Orville Redenbacher's popcorn with real butter. People recall the lit-up marquee as being a spectacular sight at night. The 700-seat theater shuttered in 1981 after screening *Alice in Wonderland* and *Swiss Family Robinson.* It was razed and is now the site of Central Park Plaza, a popular destination for concerts and ice- skating.

Courtesy of PoCo Muse

Cinema Art Theater

The Cinema Art Theater on North Main Street in Mishawaka was originally known as the Tivoli Theater. Designed by Chicago architect Edward P. Rupert and redesigned by Lawrence Monberg, it was a grand neoclassical building in the Italian Renaissance style with ornate terra-cotta. The 1,400-seat theater was the city's premier venue for vaudeville and silent films after it opened in 1925. The red-and-cream theater also housed stores and apartments. It was converted into a full-time movie theater in 1929 and was the city's most popular movie house until it closed in the 1960s. People fondly recall going there to see Roger Corman double or triple features. It was revived as the Cinema Art Theater in the late 1960s and showed adult movies until it closed in 1991. It was added to the National Register of Historic Places in 1998, and efforts were made to preserve it, but it was razed in 2005 to clear the way for the eventual development of an apartment building.

Courtesy of Cinema Treasures

MUSIC

Indiana has produced many legendary musicians, like the Jackson Five, Janet Jackson, John Mellencamp, Babyface, Kym Mazelle, Hoagy Carmichael, Wes Montgomery, Crystal Taliefero, Joshua Bell, and Blind Melon singer Shannon Hoon. The state has inspired some classic songs, like Paul Dresser's "On the Banks of the Wabash" and Professor Harold Hill's "Gary, Indiana" from *The Music Man*. More recently, Strand of Oaks released "Goshen '97" and Margot & the Nuclear So and So's "Broadripple Is Burning." Bars, restaurants, and college parties have long played Tom Petty's "Mary Jane's Last Dance" with lyrics like, "She grew up in an Indiana town/ Had a good-looking mama who never was around/ But she grew up tall and she grew up right/ With them Indiana boys on an Indiana night." The state's musical heritage echoes on in bygone venues, record labels, and nightclubs.

Courtesy of Shutterstock

Star Plaza

One of Chicagoland's largest theaters lay just across the state line in Northwest Indiana. The Star Plaza at Interstate 65 and US 30 in Merrillville hosted comedy acts like Jerry Seinfeld, George Carlin, Ellen DeGeneres, Richard Pryor, and Region native Jim Gaffigan. Howie Mandel even shot an HBO special there. Founded as the Holiday Star in 1979, the Star Plaza was an intimate venue with no seat more than 90 feet from the stage. It hosted touring Broadway shows, high school graduations, boxing, circuses, community theater, and musical acts as varied as Bob Dylan, Donna Summer, Johnny Cash, Emmylou Harris, Alice Cooper, Ministry, Ray Charles, Weird Al Yankovic, Mitzi Gaynor, Reba McEntire, and Garth Brooks. Liberace told Johnny Carson he had some of his most profitable shows there. The Oak Ridge Boys and Northwest Indiana Symphony Orchestra played Christmas concerts there every year. It was where the Region went to see acts like Second City and Itzhak Perlman before it shuttered in 2017.

Indiana Avenue

Indiana Avenue was the hub of African American commerce and cultural life in Indianapolis during the 19th century and early 20th century. A Bethel AME church first opened there in 1836. Black-owned businesses sprouted up on nearly every corner as the African American population grew. Madam C. J. Walker, the first self-made female millionaire in the country, established her cosmetics and hair products empire there. Now a US National Historic District and one of Indy's seven cultural districts, it hosted many Black nightclubs and entertainment venues that were stops on the Chitlin' Circuit. The Black Entertainment Boulevard, similar to Memphis's famed Beale Street in its heyday, hosted jazz greats like Wes Montgomery, F reddie Hubbard, and Erroll "Groundhog" Grandy. The nearly century-old Madam Walker Theatre, the avenue's crown jewel, remains a performing arts venue, but the area emptied out after residents were displaced by interstate construction, IUPUI expansion, and slum clearances between the 1950s and the 1970s.

Deer Creek

Courtesy of Wikimedia Commons

Sometimes what's lost is a name. The Deer Creek Music Center has long been the biggest venue in the Indianapolis area, bringing in top touring acts. One of the top-selling amphitheaters in the country, it's hosted bands like the Grateful Dead, Phish, Willie Nelson, John Mellencamp, and Pearl Jam over the years. The 24,790-seat outdoor amphitheater just off Interstate 69 in Noblesville still packs them in today but is now known as the Ruoff Music Center. It was Deer Creek from 1989 until 2001, when the naming rights were sold to Verizon Wireless. It's changed names several times since, shuffling from one corporate sponsor to another. The original name is lost, but almost no one is ready to let it go. As with the Sears Tower, Comiskey Park, and other renamed landmarks, it's still known as Deer Creek. There's even an "I Still Call It Deer Creek" T-shirt.

Gennett Records

Gennett Records earned Richmond the honorary title of the cradle of recorded jazz. The pioneering record label, a division of the Starr Piano Company, did some of the first jazz recordings. It recorded artists like Louis Armstrong, Jelly Roll Morton, Blind Lemon Jefferson, and Indiana's own Hoagy Carmichael. It was one of the first studios outside of New York City, one of the first to record Black artists, and one of the first to host integrated recording sessions at a time when the Ku Klux Klan ran rampant in Indiana. It also recorded blues, gospel, and country music, drawing many musicians from Kentucky, the Cincinnati Symphony Orchestra, and across the Midwest. It made albums for the Sears Catalog, radio, and film but was eventually undone by a World War II quota on shellac.

Courtesy of Wikimedia Commons

Vee-Jay Records

Vee-Jay Records in Gary was the first to release the music of the Beatles in the United States, gaining the license rights when other labels weren't interested in the boys from Liverpool. Husband-and-wife duo Vivian Carter and James C. Bracken started the record label, one of the first Black-owned labels in the country, with rehearsal space in a garage in 1953. It became a significant R&B and soul label, scoring its first billboard hit with Gary's own Spaniels. Vee-Jay Records also put out music by Jimi Hendrix, Johnny Lee Hooker, the Four Seasons, and the Pips, who would become Gladys Knight's backing group. It shuttered in 1986, and its catalog was acquired by Concord Music Group.

Courtesy of Freepik

Little Nashville Opry

The Grand Ole Opry is one of country music's most hallowed halls and the longest-running radio program in history. The Little Nashville Opry in Nashville, Indiana, didn't book chart-toppers with the same regularity but still brought in big names like Johnny Cash, Loretta Lynn, and Reba McEntire. It opened in 1975 and quickly became an institution, often running back-to-back shows that drew thousands on Saturday nights. Visitors from many other states would come to see acts like Willie Nelson or Billy Ray Cyrus, often while they were up and coming. The rustic wooden venue had pews for seating, fudge for sale, and home-cooked meals for the artists backstage. The venue burned down in 2009. Two years later, investigators charged the owners with burning it down to get $3 million in insurance money because they were so deeply in debt from their gambling addictions.

Courtesy of Elizabeth Nicodemus

Hegewisch Records

Courtesy of Ken Zurek

Hegewisch Discount started out in Chicago selling milk, nylons, batteries, and army/navy surplus. Then someone came in with a box of records that sold out in a day, General Manager and Vice President Ken Zurek recalled. Owner Joe Sotiros stocked more records, which eventually crowded everything else out. Thus was born Hegewisch Records, a legendary Calumet Region record store that grew to seven locations across Chicago's south suburbs and Northwest Indiana. In Indiana, Hegewisch Records had stores in Merrillville and Whiting, as well as the affiliated Hammond Records and Tape Exchange. It ran the Erect Records label in Merrillville. Hegewisch Records stocked over 100,000 records in genres like rock, jazz, blues, and even polka. Bands like Cheap Trick, Thin Lizzy, W.A.S.P., and Night Ranger performed in the store. It's still talked about reverently. Hegewisch Records T-shirts and memorabilia often can be found at newer record shops.

Woodmar Records

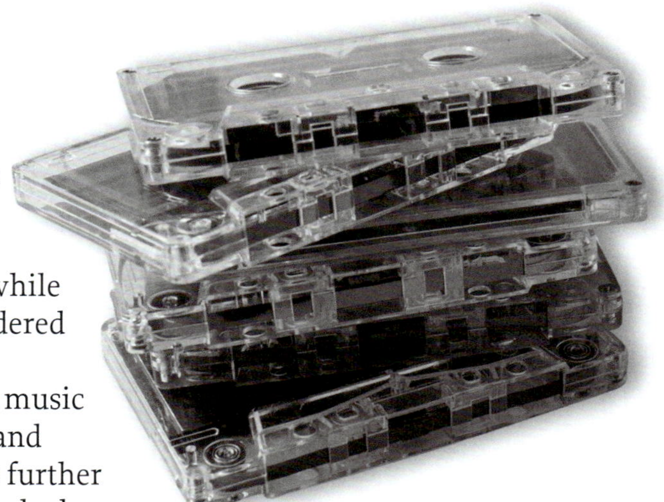
Courtesy of Freepik

Young people long flocked to Hammond's Woodmar Mall, which was designed by the pioneering Austrian mall designer Victor Gruen, to pick up new albums at Woodmar Records. It had a wide selection of rock records, stocking punk, new wave, and other genres while they were still fledgling. Its import section was considered the best around. The independent record store later expanded to Schererville, where it was run by Region music icon Tom Lounges, a promoter, DJ, radio personality, and writer who published *Midwest Beat Magazine*. To help further the local music scene he relentlessly promoted, he stocked cassettes from many local bands he knew from the nightclub circuit, like Counter Attack, Winterkill, Tyrant's Reign, Alison's Mailbox, and Gravelbone, at a time when live bands played local bars almost every night of the week. Customers lined up for midnight releases of big albums from acts like Black Sabbath.

Sunset Terrace

Courtesy of Indiana Historical Society

Indiana Avenue in downtown Indianapolis once hosted a lively jazz scene. The Sunset Terrace was a top venue there between 1937 and 1966, hosting acts like Dizzy Gillespie, the Count Basie Orchestra, Dinah Washington, Cab Calloway, B. B. King, and Lionel Hampton. The music venue at 873 Indiana Avenue was located near where the Indiana Avenue Apartments now stand. It could get a little rough. Duke Ellington once visited, got his suit sullied when people threw beer and whisky bottles toward him while fighting, and vowed he'd never return. Erroll "Groundhog" Grandy told the Indiana University History Center he wished for a bulletproof vest whenever he'd visit. None of the jazz remains, but Indiana Avenue is recognized as one of Indianapolis's Cultural Districts.

DC's Country Junction

Courtesy of Lowell Public Library

Someone called it "the night country music died" when DC's Country Junction closed in Lowell after 40 years. The roadhouse hosted line dancing and country music, including big-name performers like Luke Bryan and Merle Haggard. It had a petting zoo with peacocks, pigs, and goats and kept Siberian tigers, mountain lions, bears, monkeys, and other exotic animals in cages outside. The honky-tonk's gravel parking lot filled up with pickup trucks on weekend nights. Surrounded by cornfields, it was a regional destination that opened in 1975. People in cowboy boots and Carhartt jackets came to dance on the dusty plywood floor of the neon-lit dance hall and hear country and western acts, for instance doing call-and-responses to covers of Hank Williams Jr.'s "Family Tradition." It hosted rodeos outside, setting up bleachers out back. Near the end, it tried to draw in customers with events like mixed martial arts and midget wrestling.

LIVE ENTERTAINMENT

Every August, performers from across the country take the stage at Indy Fringe Fest, the annual theater festival on Mass Ave that's modeled after the famed Edinburgh Festival Fringe. Performers like Phil the Void put on one-man shows for roving audiences that migrate from one black-box theater to another. Thespians once captivated audiences year-round at venues like the bygone Theatre of the Dunes summer theater in Beverly Shores that brought in performers from Chicago's famed Goodman Theatre and pushed back the curtain time when the South Shore Line was running late. Back in the vaudeville days, almost every major performer passed through Indiana, but the advent of the moving picture meant curtains for many vaunted stages.

Courtesy of IMCPL

English Hotel and Opera House

Oscar Wilde once spoke at the English Hotel and Opera House on Monument Circle. The striking limestone Victorian building stood four stories tall and was adorned with spires and turrets. Captain William Hayden English built a theater and opera house that would serve as a cultural hub for about 70 years. Modeled after the New York Grand Opera House, it opened in 1880 and hosted opera, ballet, vaudeville, musical comedy, and movies. Many distinguished performers took the stage, including Sarah Bernhardt, Laurence Olivier, Tallulah Bankhead, Katharine Hepburn, and Walter Huston. In 1902, it hosted a live-action *Ben-Hur* with eight horses running on treadmills during the chariot race scene. The theater was an impressive structure with an arched proscenium, gold-and-white frescos, and two balconies. Franklin Delano Roosevelt addressed a crowd of 50,000 there in 1932. It was demolished in 1947 to make way for a JCPenney.

Courtesy of Indiana Historical Society

Mesker Park Zoo Monkey House

The Mesker Park Zoo in Evansville had a monkey ship—a replica of Christopher Columbus's *Santa Maria* at one-third scale. Zoo Director Gilmore Haynie commissioned the exhibit in 1933, and it ran for nearly 70 years. About 20 rhesus macaques as well as capuchins and lemurs monkeyed around on the ship, which was open from April to November. The monkey ship was so odd that Vladimir Nabokov alluded to it in *Lolita*. Humbert Humbert takes Lolita to Mount Rushmore, the Corn Palace in South Dakota, and "a zoo in Indiana where a large troop of monkeys lived on a concrete replica of Christopher Columbus' flagship." It was the zoo's most popular attraction. Alligators even used to swim in the moat. Today, the monkeys are kept in a more natural habitat, and the exhibit was turned into bumper boats.

Courtesy of Evansville Vanderburgh Public Library (top), Wikimedia Commons (bottom)

Circus Capital of the World

Courtesy of Library of Congress

Peru was long known as the Circus Capital of the World. Ben Wallace founded a three-ring circus that wintered in Peru for 60 years. The Great Wallace Shows initially traveled by horse and wagon and then railroad. Performers and animals wintered on a 200-acre site just off Route 124. His circus grew so large that he acquired the Carl Hagenbeck Trained Wild Animal Circus, doubling his train cars and adding 13 more elephants. The Hagenbeck-Wallace Circus rivaled the Ringling Bros. World's Greatest Shows and Barnum & Bailey's Greatest Show on Earth. The winter quarters grew to more than 150 railcars and 50 elephants. John Ringling acquired it for $1.7 million in 1929 and started closing circuses to limit competition for Ringling Bros. and Barnum & Bailey after the Great Depression. The Peru winter quarters closed in 1938. The site is now a National Historic Landmark and home to the International Circus Hall of Fame.

Bendix Woods Ski Slopes

The wooded hills of Bendix Woods County Park in New Carlisle once hosted skiing and tubing in the winter months. Skiing started on the 120-foot-tall slope when it opened as a public park in 1969 after the Bendix Corporation donated the land to St. Joseph County. It hosted ski races, downhill ski lessons, cross-country skiing, and a Winter Sports Festival. It was one of many small ski resorts on the undulating Valparaiso Moraine in Northern Indiana, including Mount Wawasee, Pines Peak in Valparaiso, and Ski Valley in La Porte, that ultimately closed. The Bendix Woods slopes shuttered in 1986 due to steep operational and insurance costs. Today, Paoli Peaks and Perfect North Slopes in Lawrenceburg are the only two remaining ski slopes in Indiana, which is not as topographically challenged as many believe but which also is not the ideal spot to find fresh powder.

Courtesy of Historic New Carlisle

Grand Theater

The massive Grand Opera House in Evansville seated 1,700 when it opened in 1889 with an orchestra balcony and second balcony. J. B. McElfatrick & Son, a leading theater architect, designed the Romanesque Revival building that housed operas, plays, and other events. It was considered the finest theater in a city that also included the Evansville Opera House, the Turner House, the Apollo, and Evans Hall. The Grand Theater was considered the city's upper- crust house and hosted presidential candidate William Howard Taft. It had started hosting touring vaudeville acts by 1910 and movies a few years later. It was renamed the Grand Theater in 1926 but continued to occasionally host live events, like the Broadway musical *Golden Boy* and the opera *La Bohème*. It showed its last film in 1962 and was razed to make way for a bank parking garage.

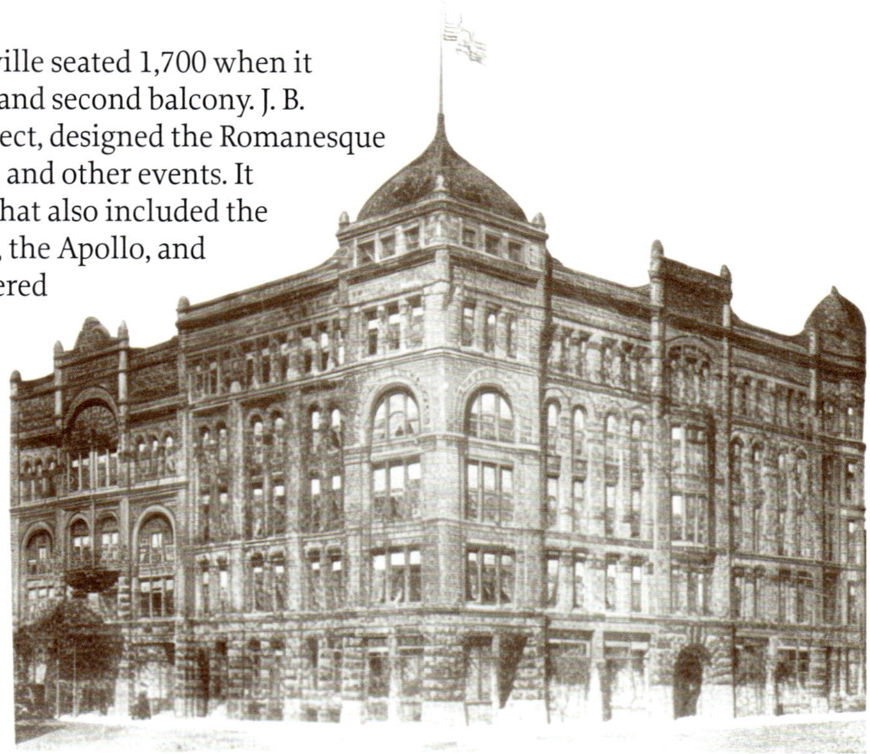

Courtesy of the Evansville Vanderburgh Public Library

Lasers on the Dunes

Michigan City used to stage a 50-minute laser show on the *Simpsons*-like hyperboloid cooling tower at the lakefront NIPSCO Generating Station on US 12. A local businessman got Stone Mountain Lasers from Georgia to stage the show at the Indiana Dunes. Stone Mountain Park outside Atlanta and Disney World had the only similar displays at the time. The show started at dusk and projected flags, geometric images, and dancing girls against the backdrop of the 200-foot-high tower. It was synced to music like the Beach Boys and Ray Charles. The gates of the coal-fired power plant opened around 5 p.m. every night so onlookers who came for the spectacle could picnic on the grounds. The site was large enough for about 10,000 people but never drew crowds anywhere near that size.

Courtesy of the Old Lighthouse Museum

Hilton U. Brown Theatre

The Hilton U. Brown Theatre, originally known as the Hilton U. Brown Theatron, entertained crowds between 1955 and 2000 at 49th Street and Boulevard Place next to Hinkle Fieldhouse on the Butler University campus. It was an open-air venue on the southern end of the Butler Bowl that was later covered to protect against the elements. Starlight Musicals staged plays there every summer for years until it folded in 1993. It also hosted college commencements and many live music acts, like Lyle Lovett, Liza Minnelli, Tears for Fears, Widespread Panic, Carol Burnett, Ziggy Marley, Tony Bennett, and Tito Puente. It was torn down in 2005 so Butler could add more parking and student housing.

Courtesy of Pixabay

Balloon Races

The first-ever race at the Indianapolis Motor Speedway, the holy grail of motorsports, did not involve cars. Hot-air balloons raced at the Brickyard for a national championship when it was still under construction in 1909. President Carl Fisher, who was the 21st person to ever earn a balloon pilot's license in the United States, wanted to recoup his investment, so he organized a balloon race for the Bennett Cup. Governor and future vice president Thomas Marshall sent off the aeronauts on a multiday race that was viewed by 40,000 spectators and won by University City out of St. Louis. Balloon races occurred regularly in the early days of the speedway and inspired Wonder Bread's name, logo, and colorful packaging. Taggart Bakery Vice President Elmer Cline was "filled with wonder" while watching the balloons take off before the Indianapolis 500 in 1921.

Red Light District

Terre Haute's Red Light District once had more than 60 brothels operated by madams between the Vigo County Courthouse and Fourth Street between Wabash Avenue and Locust Street. The West End also had gambling dens, saloons, and other spots of ill repute that earned Terre Haute its reputation as Vice City. Madame Brown's Pleasure Place was considered the crown jewel. More than 1,000 sex workers catered to out-of-towners, including Chicago mobsters. The mob first flourished in Terre Haute during Prohibition because of its location between Chicago and St. Louis. It became a gambling hub with many slots and became "the home of the largest international gambling ring ever uncovered in the US" in 1957. The Red Light District and the rest of the vice ultimately faded in the 1970s.

Pines Peak

The Pines Ski Area, also known as Pines Peak, opened in 2008. The ski hill occupied a 36-acre site at 674 Meridian near Valparaiso, where skiers and snowboarders raced down an 868-foot-tall hill. It was a small ski area with just four lifts but meant as recreation for the nearby city. Skiers could descend a 1,200-foot run. The average annual snowfall in the Lake Effect snow belt just south of Lake Michigan totaled 36 inches, but that level of snowfall failed to hold up. The Pines Ski Area closed in 2008 after 47 years after a lack of consistent snow made it impossible to run, an issue that had also killed the legendary Ogden Dunes Ski Jump decades earlier. The owner used more than 20 snowmaking machines but to no avail. It was abandoned but started luring the morbidly curious and mountain bikers drawn to its hilly terrain.

Maennerchor Club

Courtesy of Indiana Historical Society

In 1854, German immigrants got together to found the Indianapolis Maennerchor, a men's choir and social club. Others popped up in Pittsburgh and Cincinnati. The Indianapolis chapter built the three-and-a-half-story 40,000-square-foot Maennerchor Building at the corner of Illinois and Michigan Streets downtown. It was designed by Adolph Scherrer, who also did the Indiana State Capitol and the Crown Hill Cemetery gateway. Dignitaries like James Whitcomb Riley and Vice President Charles W. Fairbanks attended the opening. The Maennerchor Building hosted regular concerts from touring artists like the Budapest String Quartet in its 800-seat auditorium. It was renamed the Academy of Music Building during World War I, when anti-German sentiment ran high. The Maennerchor Building became a Service Men's Center, a nightclub, and Indiana University's Indianapolis Law School before it was demolished and turned into a parking lot. The choir performed for the last time at Victory Field in 2018.

La Porte Theatre

The French Renaissance–style La Porte Theatre was an entertainment destination for a half century, hosting vaudeville acts, staging plays, and screening films. Designed by Chicago architect Henry L. Newhouse, the 1,576-seat auditorium on Lincolnway opened in 1923 and featured a Wurlitzer Organ. Some called it the pride of La Porte. Sweeping across an entire city block, it housed shops, businesses, and the Lincoln Hotel upstairs. Some significant names performed there over the years, including Ethel Barrymore and Otis Skinner. The opulent interior also made it a venue for La Porte High School proms for years. The theater was demolished in the late 1970s to make way for a bank.

Courtesy of the La Porte County Historian

Courtesy of the La Porte County Historian

Phoenix Theatre

The Phoenix Theatre was a hub for entertainment in La Porte in the late 19th century and early 20th century. The playhouse at Lincolnway and Clay Street was known by many names over the years, like the Opera House, Huntsman Hall, and Lay's Hall. The Phoenix Theatre was built in 1858, remodeled after a few years, and rebuilt after fires in 1875 and 1909. It was turned into a movie house after the 1909 fire. That renovation removed street-level storefronts like Steinberg Jewelers and added a second-floor dance house. It hosted three vaudeville shows a night while also screening moving pictures. The building was remodeled into a store and an office in 1924 and later razed.

Courtesy of Johnson's Indy 500

Balloon Spectacle

For more than 70 years, multicolored, helium-filled balloons were released into the heavens as part of the prerace festivities at the Indianapolis 500. Owner Anton "Tony" Hulman started the "Balloon Spectacle" tradition sometime after buying the Indianapolis Motor Speedway in 1945. The balloons were released from a tent in the infield moments before the race during the rendition of "Back Home Again in Indiana" when the singer reached the lyric "the new-mown hay sends all its fragrance." The wind would carry off the balloons, which usually remained visible from the grandstands for about 20 minutes. As with balloon releases nationwide, the practice came under fire from environmentalists who were concerned about littering so much nonbiodegradable plastic across the countryside. The Indianapolis Motor Speedway announced in 2022 it was pausing the balloon release, which had last taken place in 2019 before COVID-19.

Terre Haute Grand Opera House

The Terre Haute Grand Opera House opened in 1897 at North Seventh Street and Cherry Street, where the Naylor Opera House stood before it was destroyed in a fire. The 1,300-seat venue hosted not just opera but plays, concerts, and other performances at a time when Terre Haute was the entertainment hub of Western Indiana. John Philip Sousa, Al Jolson, and Ethel Barrymore were among the many entertainers to take the stage there. It was renamed the Grand Theatre in the 1930s when movies usurped live entertainment. It showed movies like *Gone with the Wind* but closed in 1959 and was razed the next year.

Courtesy of Vigo County History Center

MUSEUMS

Indiana boasts a wealth of museums, like Newfields, the Indiana State Museum, the Fort Wayne Museum of Art, and the Eiteljorg Museum of American Indians and Western Art. The Indianapolis Children's Museum is the largest in the world and is considered one of the country's finest. IU, Notre Dame, and Ball State University all have fine art museums. Elkhart has the RV/MH Hall of Fame & Museum, South Bend the Indiana Dinosaur Museum, and Evansville the riverfront Evansville Museum of Arts, History & Science. One can board a decommissioned USS *LST-325* tank carrier on the Ohio River in Evansville or explore museums dedicated to figures like Kurt Vonnegut, Ernie Pyle, Eugene Debs, and Lew Wallace. But the exhibition halls have closed at museums across the state, including auto, aviation, and other specialty museums.

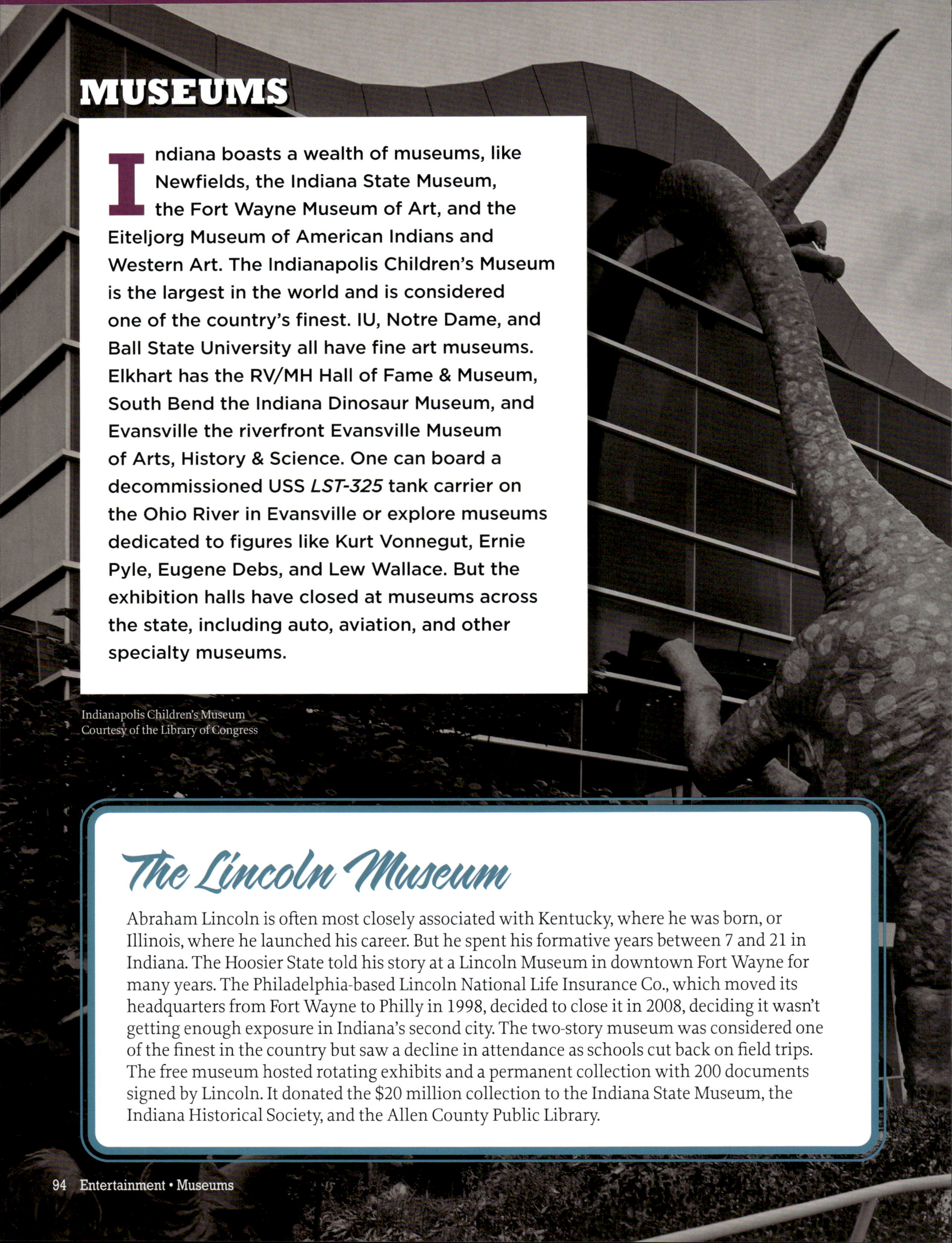

Indianapolis Children's Museum
Courtesy of the Library of Congress

The Lincoln Museum

Abraham Lincoln is often most closely associated with Kentucky, where he was born, or Illinois, where he launched his career. But he spent his formative years between 7 and 21 in Indiana. The Hoosier State told his story at a Lincoln Museum in downtown Fort Wayne for many years. The Philadelphia-based Lincoln National Life Insurance Co., which moved its headquarters from Fort Wayne to Philly in 1998, decided to close it in 2008, deciding it wasn't getting enough exposure in Indiana's second city. The two-story museum was considered one of the finest in the country but saw a decline in attendance as schools cut back on field trips. The free museum hosted rotating exhibits and a permanent collection with 200 documents signed by Lincoln. It donated the $20 million collection to the Indiana State Museum, the Indiana Historical Society, and the Allen County Public Library.

College Football Hall of Fame

The College Football Hall of Fame was supposed to open in 1949 in New Jersey, where Rutgers and Princeton played the first-ever college football game in 1869. Despite years of fundraising, it never took root in the Garden State. It finally was built in 1978 in suburban Cincinnati next to the Kings Island amusement park, but failed to draw. It relocated in 1991 to South Bend, the home of the Notre Dame Fighting Irish that beat out 35 other cities. The $14 million museum near Century Center had an artificial turf field with regulation goalposts outside and interactive exhibits about blocking and other skills. It drew only about 60,000 visitors a year instead of the projected 150,000. It closed at the end of 2012 before relocating to Atlanta in another sign of how the center of gravity in the college football universe has shifted to SEC territory.

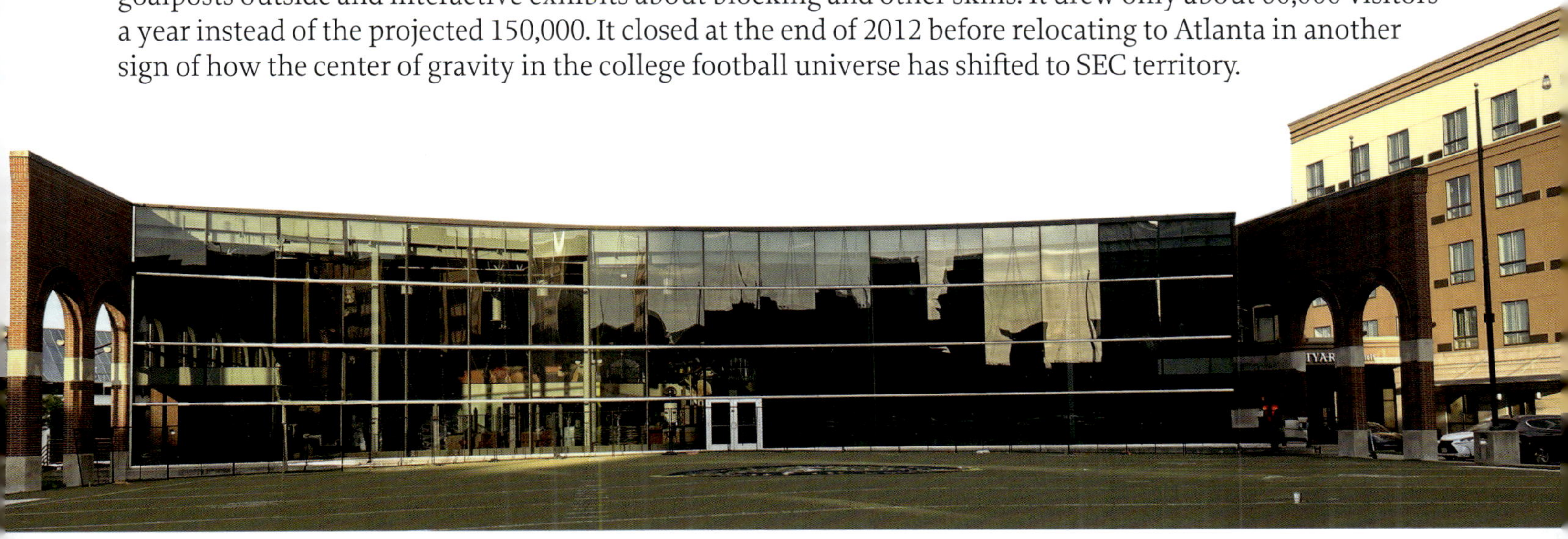

Clabber Girl Museum

Courtesy of Wikimedia Commons

Clabber Girl is one of the best known and most enduring name-brand consumer goods to emerge from the Hoosier State. Hulman & Company, which owned the Indianapolis Motor Speedway and the IndyCar racing league, long made Clabber Girl baking powder, baking soda, and cornstarch. Founded in the mid-1800s, the company blended clabbered milk with pearl ash to make the kitchen staple Clabber Girl Double-Action Baking Powder. Named after sour milk, Clabber Girl ran Indiana's only baking museum at its Terre Haute headquarters until it was shut down in 2022. The museum featured a demonstration kitchen, a replica grocery store, a saloon, a Victorian parlor, and a racing exhibit highlighting the Hulman family's long history with motorsports after buying the Indianapolis Motor Speedway from World War I flying ace Eddie Rickenbacker. It also boasted a community art gallery, a bake shop, a café, and a gift shop selling Clabber Girl products.

Mascot Hall of Fame

The Phillie Phanatic, Phoenix Gorilla, and other mascots delighted kids and sports fans of all ages at the Mascot Hall of Fame in Whiting. The interactive children's museum was tucked between Lake Michigan and the hulking BP Whiting Refinery from late 2018 to 2024. The building was designed to resemble a giant mascot who was clutching a jumbotron-sized billboard in one hand and who had a giant booger big enough to crush a Buick dangling from its nose. Kids who came in for field trips would come in the lobby, look up, and marvel at the giant mascot heads above in the three-story museum that drew visitors from all 50 states and across the globe. *USA Today* 10Best named it the No. 1 Pop Culture Museum in the United States. It displayed more than 2,000 artifacts from professional and collegiate mascots, and mascots like Benny the Bull made frequent visits.

John Dillinger Museum

Crime doesn't pay, a sign warned visitors to the John Dillinger Museum. The museum was originally located in the Indiana Welcome Center in Hammond and was later moved to the Old Lake County Courthouse basement in downtown Crown Point before closing abruptly in 2017. The museum told the story of the Depression-era bank robber who captured the public imagination at a time when people hated banks. He had strong connections to Northwest Indiana, where he often hid out while robbing banks and police stations across the Midwest. He stayed in the Indiana State Prison in Michigan City, robbed the First National Bank in East Chicago, and infamously escaped from the Crown Point Jail with a wooden gun he had whittled in his cell. The museum displayed artifacts like a Public Enemy Number One wanted poster, a Tommy gun, a lucky rabbit foot, and a replica Biograph Theater marquee.

Courtesy of Indiana Aviation Museum

Indiana Aviation Museum

The former US Marine Corps pilot Jim Read collected warbirds for nearly a decade before opening his own museum in the Porter County Regional Airport in Valparaiso. The Indiana Aviation Museum took flight in 2001. It displayed a variety of planes, like the Beechcraft T-34B Mentor, the Cessna A-37A Dragonfly, the North American T-28B Trojan, and the Taylorcraft L-2 Grasshopper, even offering rides in some of them. The museum organized the annual Porter County Heritage Air Show until its T-28 crashed into a creek after overrunning the runway in 2007. The Indiana Aviation Museum lasted a decade but eventually shuttered due to rising costs. The planes were sold off. Most of the artifacts went to the Grissom Air Museum or the Hoosier Air Museum, which itself closed in 2019.

Ropkey Armor Museum

Courtesy of John Schanlaub via Wikimedia Commons

The Ropkey Armor Museum shuttered in Crawfordsville after 35 years in 2017. Former Marine Corps tank commander Fred Ropkey, a Korean War veteran and avid military historian, opened the museum to display an array of historic military vehicles like tanks, Bradley Fighting Vehicles, jeeps, boats, and aircraft that was hailed as "one of the finest private collections in the country." He lent some of them out to Hollywood productions like *The Blues Brothers* and *Tank*. He started young, getting his first World War I sword and Civil War pistol as gifts from his parents when he was just 8 years old. As a teen, he bought his own World War II scout car that he drove to school. He established the museum "in a little pole barn on a 50-acre cornfield" in Crawfordsville, telling WISH-TV "everything in the museum runs, flies, or floats, but the cannons don't fire."

ART

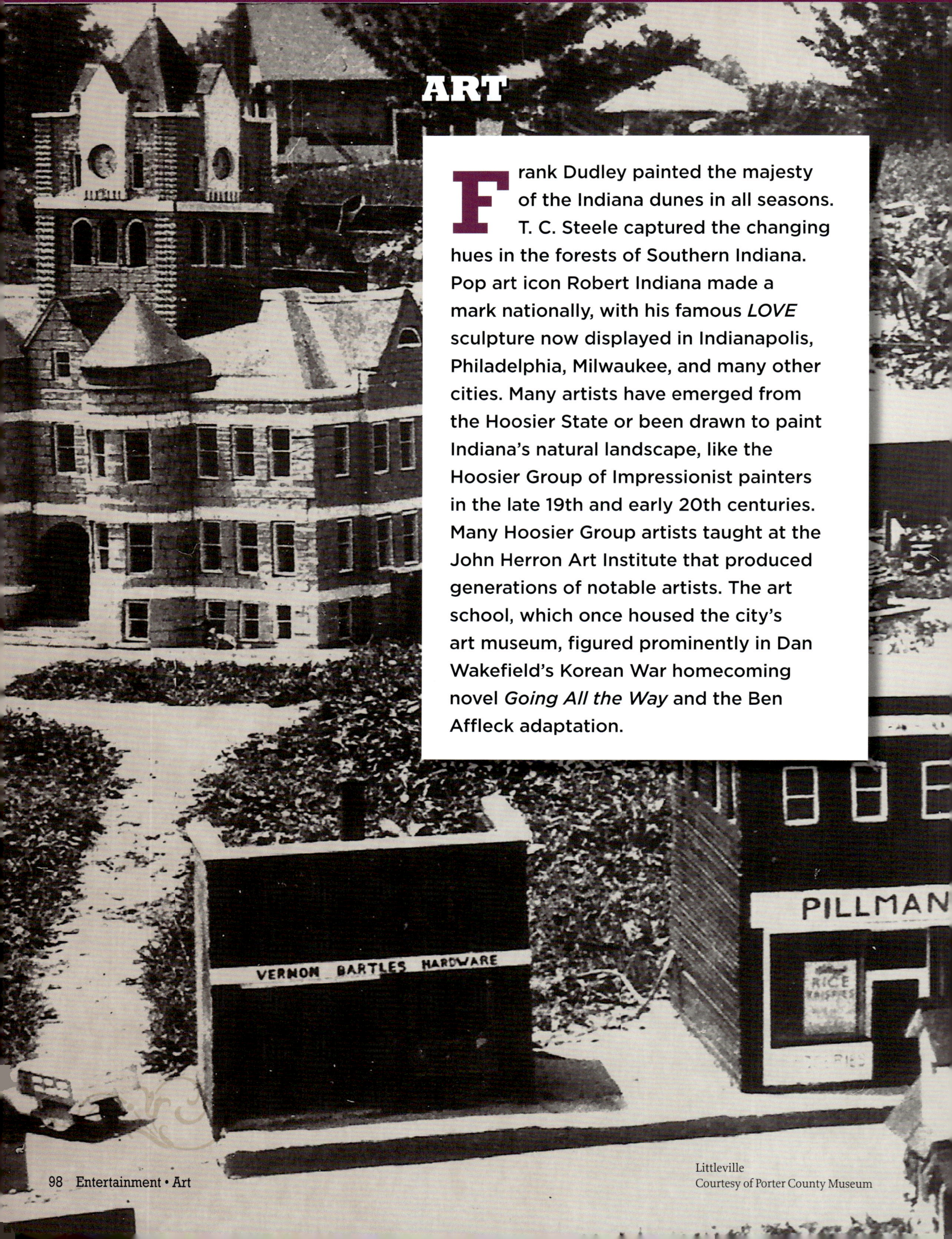

Frank Dudley painted the majesty of the Indiana dunes in all seasons. T. C. Steele captured the changing hues in the forests of Southern Indiana. Pop art icon Robert Indiana made a mark nationally, with his famous *LOVE* sculpture now displayed in Indianapolis, Philadelphia, Milwaukee, and many other cities. Many artists have emerged from the Hoosier State or been drawn to paint Indiana's natural landscape, like the Hoosier Group of Impressionist painters in the late 19th and early 20th centuries. Many Hoosier Group artists taught at the John Herron Art Institute that produced generations of notable artists. The art school, which once housed the city's art museum, figured prominently in Dan Wakefield's Korean War homecoming novel *Going All the Way* and the Ben Affleck adaptation.

Littleville
Courtesy of Porter County Museum

Brown County Art Colony

Brown County draws countless leaf peepers, hikers, and nature enthusiasts, especially when the colors of its tree canopies turn in its capacious forests every fall. In the late 19th and early 20th centuries, it drew many landscape painters who sought to capture its natural beauty. The artist colony included William McKendree Snyder, Evelynne Mess Daily, Alexis J. Fournier, Marie Goth, Carl Graf, and other noted artists. Most notably, it attracted T. C. Steele, who built a home and studio on an isolated hilltop west of town where he did impressionist paintings of the surrounding woods. He was considered the dean of Indiana painters and was the best known of the Hoosier Group. The professor at nearby Indiana University exhibited his work internationally, gaining widespread acclaim.

Littleville

Littleville was a miniature kingdom in downtown Chesterton built by steelworker William Murray. The eight-foot-tall town featured a castle, baseball stadium, school, hotels, churches, airport, cemeteries, feed store, movie theater, lighthouse, and oil refinery. It drew up to 133,000 visitors a year in the 1930s and 1940s. They paid five cents for a tour and two more cents for a souvenir copy of the *Littleville News* newspaper. The attraction also sold postcards depicting its miniature buildings and streets. Littleville was closed during World War II because of a rubber shortage that made it hard to procure the raw material needed to maintain it. It was torn down and replaced with actual homes, but the ruins of the small castle remain in a resident's backyard as one of its last traces.

Courtesy of Porter County Museum

iMOCA

The Indianapolis Museum of Contemporary Art or iMOCA did some cool events, like a sleepover *Twin Peaks* marathon, when it was located in Fountain Square. Later known as Indianapolis Contemporary, it started in 2001 as a "museum without walls" hosting exhibits around the city, including at Indiana Landmarks, Cat Head Press, and the Hoosier Art Salon. It had transitory homes in the Emelie Building, Murphy Arts Center, and the Alexander hotel at CityWay. It finally found what it hoped would become a permanent home in an old Ford assembly plant on Washington Street on the near east side. But it struggled with fundraising challenges and later the pandemic, closing for good in 2020. It had hosted more than 40 exhibits featuring 75 different artists over the years. Its closure left Indy as one of the largest cities in the country without a contemporary art museum.

Courtesy of Wikimedia Commons

Castle Gallery

The Castle Gallery in Fort Wayne occupied a literal castle. The businessman B. Paul Mossman built the imposing structure as a wedding present for his wife in 1905. Masons crafted the magnificent Richardsonian Romanesque residence with boulders found in fields for hundreds of miles around, fashioning the interior with hardwoods like cherry, oak, walnut, and maple. He donated it to the city to host its art museum in 1949. The Fort Wayne Museum of Art moved downtown in 1983, and the building became a home again. The 7,000-square-foot castle on West Wayne Street in the West Central neighborhood was turned into the Castle Gallery in 1995. It ended up closing after founder Jody Hemphill Smith died in late 2023, closing the next year after three decades.

Herron Art Institute

The farmer and real estate investor John Herron made a major donation to fund the John Herron Art Institute at 16th and Pennsylvania Streets in downtown Indianapolis. In 1902, the institute opened an art museum and Indiana's oldest and largest art school. Artists like Brandt Steele and Virginia Keep taught day, evening, and weekend classes that often focused on arts and crafts and applied arts. The Herron School of Art and Design became part of Indiana University in 1967, then Indiana University–Purdue University Indianapolis, and then Indiana University Indianapolis. It was originally located in the Tinker House and then a three-story neoclassical building designed by Vonnegut & Bohn. Philadelphia architect Paul Philippe Cret added to the campus by building a beaux arts–style main building, which was linked by a walkway to the brutalist Fesler Hall that was built decades later. Herron students won the Prix de Rome four straight years in the 1930s. The museum built a collection that included Van Gogh, O'Keefe, Seurat, and Cezanne before leaving the campus and spinning off into the Indianapolis Museum of Art in 1970.

Courtesy of Wikimedia Commons

Ruschman Art Gallery

The Ruschman Art Gallery started displaying contemporary art in 1985. Mark Ruschman founded the gallery in the Massachusetts Avenue neighborhood in Indianapolis, helping rejuvenate the corridor. It exhibited local and regional artists and was considered one of the most successful art galleries downtown due to its quality and professionalism. It was part of the First Friday Art Tour since it started. The gallery moved to Alabama Street in 1996, remaining a mainstay in the downtown Indy arts scene known for supporting local artists. It closed in 2009, just shy of its 25th anniversary during the Great Recession at a time when art collecting hit a nadir as collectors' wealth dried up.

{RETAIL}

Indiana once had many grand department stores, including the famed L. S. Ayres in downtown Indianapolis, Wolf & Dessauer in Fort Wayne, and Goldblatt's in Hammond, which inspired Jean Shepherd to write the department store and Santa scenes in *A Christmas Story*. It's a common misconception that Shepherd, the raconteur and radio host who built a cult following of "Night People" while hosting the late-night show on New York City's WOR live from a café in Greenwich Village, cameoed as Santa in the film adaptation of his book *In God We Trust: All Others Pay Cash*. The actor Jeff Gillen actually kicked the Red Ryder BB gun–crazed Ralphie down the slide at Higbee's Department Store, which was modeled after Shepherd's experiences shopping in downtown Hammond as a kid. Shepherd provided the voice-over for the Christmas classic that airs around the clock on cable during the holiday and that relates his often embellished stories of growing up under the shadow of steel mills in Northwest Indiana. The Hammond he grew up in is hardly recognizable today due to the wrecking ball that cleared away sites like the Cam Lan Restaurant that inspired the Peking duck scene.

Across the Hoosier State, department stores have since dwindled, shopping malls have emptied out, and landmark pharmacy chains have gotten swallowed up by larger competitors. Hoosiers cherish fond memories of heading downtown to shop, staying at swanky hotels, and bumming around at malls that fell victim to the wrecking ball. It's easier than ever to place orders online, but e-commerce will never compare to the memories people made while shopping in the brick-and-mortar stores of yesteryear, whether beholding extravagant Christmas window displays, lining up for a new record release, or browsing a video store on a Friday night.

Columbia Hotel, Greenfield
Courtesy of Hancock County Historical Society

Osborn Hotel
Courtesy of Culver Academies Museum

Lakeview Hotel
Courtesy of Culver Academies Museum

RETAIL STORES

Glaciers once plowed over Indiana, making the terrain fertile. Agriculture dominated the state's early development, and Indiana became dotted with small towns between the farmland. Farmers came to town to shop for sundries, and local shops thrived, often on downtown squares surrounding county courthouses. Industry arrived, helping create many midsize cities like Muncie, Anderson, and Columbus. They were shopping hubs with grand department stores that catered to every conceivable need. Postwar suburbanization greatly shifted shopping habits, moving the shopping hubs to highways on the outskirts of town. Shoppers flocked to malls, strip malls, and big-box stores as national chains took over. The downtowns that fostered so many homegrown independent retailers never completely died but are no longer the center of gravity for shoppers.

King's Grocery

King's Grocery in Bristol was long known as the Old Store as it dated back to 1841, just six years after the town was founded. Located next to the opera house, it burned down in 1846 and was rebuilt two years later. It was owned by H. B. App during the early 20th century, when it was a dry goods store that sold sundries like shoes, boots, caps, clothes, and tools. It evolved into a grocery store after refrigeration and transportation improved enough for such stores to sell perishable goods. Augustus King acquired the Old Store in 1925. It burned down in 2024 after 176 years.

Courtesy of Freepik

Butt Drugs

Courtesy of Wikimedia Commons

Butt Drugs sounds like a way of describing a diaper rash ointment that would crack up a toddler, a back alley for smuggling contraband into a prison, or a shortcut to shaping one's posterior that would be banned by most sports governing associations. But it's more than just a cheap laugh. The independent family-owned pharmacy and old-timey soda fountain was part of the fabric of Corydon for 71 years. Founded by pharmacist William Butt in 1952, the 2,900-square-foot store lasted three generations before closing in 2023 due to financial struggles partly brought on by insurance payments that lowered reimbursement rates, according to the *Corydon Democrat.* The inadvertently funny drugstore sold "I Love Butt Drugs" T-shirts as well as magazines, Troll dolls, and Whitman's Chocolates.

The Big Store

Muncie was once known as Little Chicago in part because of its dense downtown that bustled with shoppers. The Magic City was home to many shopping options. In the 1870s, George Stephenson and B. G. Braxton opened a dry-goods store downtown, moving it to the Odd Fellows Building before selling it to O. A. Johnson, who sold it to William Alonzo McNaughton, who had a flair for salesmanship. He moved it to the new Johnson-Morgan Building, where it gained the nickname "the Big Store" and stocked a fine assortment of home goods, cookware, and clothes like a $3.50 double beaver cape. In 1903, it expanded into a five-story, 100,000-square-foot building made of Indiana limestone, Vermont granite, and Ohio pressed brick.

Ball Stores

Courtesy of Delaware County Historical Society

Muncie's "Big Store" went bankrupt during the Great Depression and was purchased by the Ball Brothers Corporation. The first family of Muncie believed the store should be saved, just as it rescued Ball State University predecessor Eastern Indiana Normal School, fearing it would go dark or be sold to an outside chain. They converted it into the flagship of the Ball Stores department store chain, a locally beloved shopping destination known for its brown plaid motif and high-quality merchandise. The Ball Stores expanded to more locations during the 1960s, including in the Village and the Muncie Malls. All its locations had shuttered by 1990, when Elder-Beerman took over the last remaining location at the mall.

Marsh Supermarkets

Generations shopped for groceries at Marsh Supermarkets in Central Indiana. The local chain started in 1931 in Muncie but was later headquartered in Indianapolis. It grew to a height of 97 locations throughout Indiana and Ohio, including Cincinnati, employing as many as 9,000 people. Ermal Marsh founded the retailer during the Great Depression, running stores under the brands Marsh, O'Malia's Food Market, and MainStreet Markets. The company went public in 1953 and opened the chain of Village Pantry convenience stores that had as many as 400 locations before going under. Marsh was an early adopter of new technology, including barcode scanners, customer loyalty programs, and co-branded Visas. The chain folded in 2017 due in part to competition from larger retailers like Kroger and Walmart that had more buying power to offer lower prices. One of its first barcode scanners is enshrined in the Smithsonian's National Museum of American History in Washington, DC.

Courtesy of Wikimedia Commons

Fetla's Trading Post

Courtesy of PoCo Muse

The Fetla's Trading Post was an unusual shopping destination for more than 90 years. The massive retailer opened in 1915 on Indiana 2 in Valparaiso. It began as a one-stop place for shopping long before Walmart arrived on the scene. The 30,000-square-foot store sold sporting goods, fishing rods, paddleboats, hardware, haircuts, clothes, and dish and dinette sets. "Fetla's was this place where you could buy a bear trap, an Uzi, a horse saddle, a bicycle, some cabinets, a pontoon boat, nunchucks, a stereo, blue jeans, a loaf of bread, a pack of cigarettes, and a gallon of milk," one customer fondly recalled. "It was absolutely off the hook, kinda like a Walmart Superstore for preppers. When I was 14, I used some of my detasseling money to buy a bullwhip and some throwing knives. It was glorious." It closed in Valpo in 2008 and later at its satellite location in Knox, which was much smaller.

The Hole

There are many notable construction pits, like the Spire in Chicago, Oceanwide Center in San Francisco, the Pit of Despair in Asheville, and the Burlington Hole in Vermont. For nearly a decade, an empty hole yawned in downtown South Bend where a redevelopment project never came to fruition. The city cleared away properties on the east side of Michigan Street between Washington and Colfax, razing the Philadelphia Restaurant and Sally Swiss Cafeteria. The redevelopment commission wanted to build a mall and office complex that never materialized. It came to be known around town as the Hole. It hosted the city's bicentennial fireworks in 1976 and was used to dump snow from the infamous blizzard of 1978. First Source Bank built the landmark glass-and-steel First Source Bank Center there in 1980.

Haag Drugs

Haag Drugs was a drugstore, apothecary, malt shop, and toy store that had locations across Indianapolis. The German brothers Louis and Julius Haag opened the flagship location on Massachusetts Avenue in 1876 with the slogan "Cut Price Drugs." They bought directly from the manufacturer, prioritizing volume over margin. They grew to multiple locations and sold many elixirs, like Wine of Cardui, Swamp Root, and Sloan's Liniment. They also sold whisky they claimed was for medicinal purposes during Prohibition but got charged with bootlegging in 1920. The liquor was dumped into the sewer, and they were sent to federal prison. New ownership took over the pharmacy, which grew across Central Indiana. It sold toys, kids' clothes, cameras, cigars, soda, hobby supplies, perfume, and Hoosier Air Lift gift packages for soldiers in Vietnam. It was acquired in 1979 by Toledo-based Peoples Drug, which in turn was bought by CVS.

Hook's Drug Stores

Hook's Drug Stores was a staple in the Indianapolis area for much of the 20th century. Founded by pharmacist John A. Hook, it had grown to a dozen locations by 1912. Kurt Vonnegut Sr., the famed author's father, designed most of its stores. Hook's Drug Stores grew rapidly after World War II, adding 150 new locations between 1946 and 1972. It operated stores under the Hook's, Brooks, and SupeRX brands. It was bought out by Kroger and then Revco, which got swallowed up by CVS. Most of its former stores are now CVS locations. Every year during the Indiana State Fair, people visit a restored 1849 Hook's Drug Store with vintage 19th-century cabinets at the Indiana State Fairgrounds. It's now a museum where you can find kidney root, Peruvian celery, and Dr. Pierce's Favorite Prescription "for the cure of those chronic weaknesses and complaints peculiar to females."

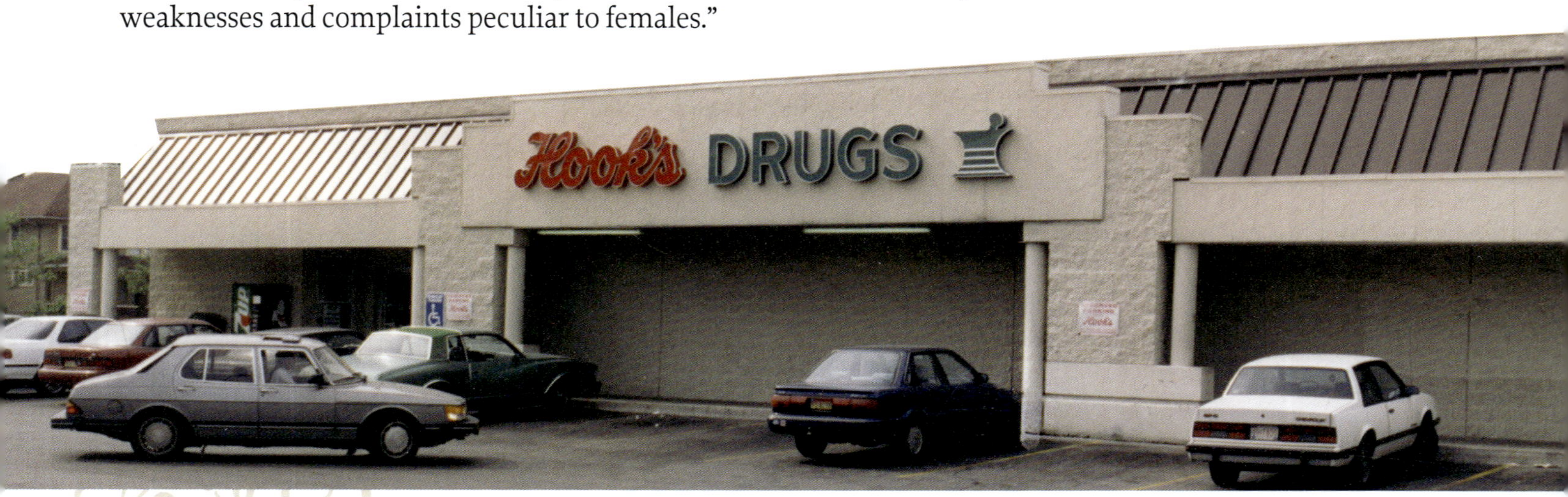

Courtesy of Indiana Historical Society

DEPARTMENT STORES

For 85 years, people dressed up to dine at the L. S. Ayres Tea Room at the grand department store known for offering "That Ayres Look." The formal tearoom opened in 1905 at Washington and Meridian Streets in downtown Indianapolis. It had expanded by 1929, moving from the fifth floor to the eighth floor. People wore hats, gloves, and their Sunday best while going to celebrate formal occasions. It was so popular that it was revived with a smaller replica at the Indiana State Museum long after the department store closed. It fills up around the holidays. Department stores around the state used to provide that type of elegance and elevated experience, but the department stores of yesteryear have been struggling everywhere as shopping habits have changed.

Ayres Building
Courtesy of IMCPL

L. S. Ayres and Company

Vonnegut and Bohn, the architecture firm run by Kurt Vonnegut's grandfather, Bernard, designed L. S. Ayres and Company, downtown Indy's venerable department store. It was founded by Lyman S. Ayres in 1872 and became known for its Christmas displays, basement budget store, and famous Tea Room, a replica of which lives on in the Indiana State Museum. The eight-story store had the slogan "That Ayres Look." L. S. Ayres was acquired by Associated Dry Goods in 1972, closed stores after the May Company bought it in 1986, and shuttered its flagship Indy location in 1992. As was the case with so many other department stores across the country, the remaining Ayres stores became Macy's in 2006.

L. Strauss and Co.

Indianapolis 500 winners used to get celebratory milk, the chance to kiss the bricks, the Borg-Warner Trophy, and the L. Strauss & Co. Trophy. L. Strauss & Co. was an upscale department store chain that was headquartered in Indianapolis during its 140-year run. It was known as the Eagle Clothing Company when it was founded in 1853 but was renamed after Leopold Strauss when he bought it in 1879. Its flagship store was in the Occidental Building at Washington and Illinois Streets in downtown Indianapolis, but the structure was torn down so the Circle Centre Mall could be built. It was supposed to reopen in the downtown Indy mall and blamed construction delays when it filed for bankruptcy and went under in 1993.

Courtesy of Indiana Historical Society

Meis Department Store

Courtesy of Vigo County History Center

The Meis department store chain started in downtown Terre Haute in 1928. Lucien Meis and Salo Levite founded the retailer, which grew to four stores in Terre Haute and expanded to other markets like Anderson, Kokomo, Marion, and Elkhart. The chain billed itself as "the fashion center of the Wabash Valley." It eventually grew to 1,600 employees and 11 stores in Indiana, Illinois, and Kentucky. It also had a jeans store called the Bottom Half. The flagship store at 624 Wabash Avenue was the last remaining department store in downtown Terre Haute, but it shuttered in 1972. The chain stayed in business with its mall locations until 1989, when it was sold to Elder-Beerman.

William H. Block Co.

The William H. Block Company department store was located across from the Indianapolis Traction Terminal, where visitors arrived on interurbans from across Indiana. Austro-Hungarian immigrant Herman Wilhelm Bloch launched the company in 1874. Vonnegut & Bohn designed an eight-story store that opened in 1911 on the corner of Illinois and Market Streets, and it was declared the "pride of Hoosierdom." It doubled in size in 1934 and claimed to be "one of the country's most beautiful department stores" with stainless steel escalators, marble facades, and a modern style. It operated restaurants like the Fountain Luncheonette, the Terrace Tea Room, and the James Whitcomb Riley Room. Indiana's second-largest retailer after L. S. Ayres, Block grew to a peak of 10 locations, including in Broad Ripple and Bloomington's College Mall, before it was acquired by Federated Department Stores in 1987. Most stores were rebranded as Lazarus. The flagship store closed in 1993.

Courtesy of Wikimedia Commons

Wyman's Department Store

Founded by an Ohio transplant, George Wyman and Company served shoppers for 112 years, including for nearly 100 years at its landmark spot on Michigan Street in downtown South Bend, which opened in 1878. Wyman's Department Store billed itself as "The Home of a Thousand Useful Gifts" and carried all manner of dry goods before evolving into a full-service department store. It cut window shades, made hats, and offered home delivery throughout Michiana. It expanded when it bought the Ellsworth Department Store next door in 1951 and added five more additions in 1962, including its signature blue and white ceramic tile facade. It wowed pedestrians with its brightly lit window displays and hosted annual teas for longtime customers. The landmark department store shuttered in 1972 and was torn down the next year to make way for redevelopment. It's now a parking lot next to Cafe Navarre.

LOWENSTINE'S Department Store

Courtesy of PoCo Muse

For more than a century, shoppers came to downtown Valparaiso to shop at Lowenstine's Department Store and later the Highland Downtown Store before a fire leveled it in 1996. The department stores both occupied a huge three-story white building on the Porter County Courthouse Square. It was the first store in Valparaiso to have a parking lot and the first with a self-serve grocery. Lowenstine's was a general-purpose store and eventually withered due to competition. The Highland Department Store replaced it in 1987 but used only half of the building and closed within seven years. Renovation plans were dashed after the fire.

Grand Leader/Stillman's

The Grand Leader department store opened in downtown Fort Wayne in 1913. The department store was part of a chain John Stillman ran in Michigan and Indiana. It hopped around until it found a long-term home in a seven-story Art Deco building on Calhoun and Wayne in 1928. The architect A. M. Strauss designed the white terra-cotta zigzag-style building. Stillman moved the headquarters of his company from Saginaw to Fort Wayne before merging with Interstate Department Stores and relocating to New York City, where the wholesalers were located. He bought up retail stores across the country, including the toy stores Children's Supermart and Children's Bargain Town that were merged into Toys "R" Us. His Fort Wayne store was rebranded as Stillman's and opened a second location at the Southgate Mall in 1955. Both locations closed in the 1970s.

Courtesy of Allen County Public Library

Wolf & Dessauer

Courtesy of Allen County Public Library

Wolf & Dessauer was where Fort Wayne went to shop from 1896 on. Parents took kids there for back-to-school clothes. It had a hair salon, a lunch counter, and a wide variety of general merchandise. The department store was especially beloved for its Christmas window displays it unveiled every year on Thanksgiving. It put out a Merry Christmas wreath, Santa with his reindeer, and a rotating array of animated scenes that often featured animatronic elves. It burned down in the 1960s.

Calhoun Christmas Tree Arch

Courtesy of Allen County Public Library

The Calhoun Christmas Tree Arch long spread holiday cheer in downtown Fort Wayne. A Christmas tree with a star on top and large ball ornaments was placed on arches and later a pedestrian archway over Calhoun Street near the Murphy Co. and Wolf & Dessauer department stores, which had Christmas window displays that some claimed rivaled those of stores in Chicago and New York City. Fort Wayne first placed the "Spirit of Christmas" pine tree over Calhoun and Wayne Streets in 1960. The majestic tree became a beloved holiday tradition, towering over the busy downtown street so cars and pedestrians could pass underneath. It was discontinued in 2008, but then Flagstar Bank brought back a 25-foot-tall Christmas tree in 2019 for Fort Wayne's annual Night of Lights celebration. It's also when the giant Merry Christmas wreath is illuminated on the side of the Indiana Michigan Power building in another long-running festive holiday tradition.

MALLS

Indiana is home to Simon Property Group, the largest US mall operator. It helped Indianapolis develop the downtown Circle Centre Mall, whose trajectory reflects that of malls across the state. Downtown Indy had declined as a shopping destination by the 1980s. So the city developed a four-story mall spanning two city blocks while maintaining the facades of the existing urban streetscape. The L. S. Ayres and William H. Block department stores closed before the mall opened, but it still thrived early on with 99 shops, a Regal multiplex, and the Nordstrom and Parisian anchors. It's plugged vacancies over the years with nontraditional uses like Brown Mackie College and the *Indianapolis Star* newsroom. After years of decline, a redevelopment project kicked off in 2025 to reimagine the mall to be more mixed-use with outdoor space, offices, and apartments.

Courtesy of Freepik

Pembroke Arcade

Courtesy of the Indiana Historical Society

The Pembroke Arcade was Indianapolis's first mall. Henry M. Talbott and George A. Dickson were inspired to spend more on an ornate building after a visit to England. Vonnegut & Bohn designed the building, which was described as strikingly beautiful when it opened in 1895. The modern Renaissance-style building with marble terrazzo mosaic floors and a high-arched glass roof drew comparisons to arcades in London, Paris, and Milan. It featured 28 shops, Italian terra-cotta shields, and a large archway topped by a gilded cupola made of hammered copper in the Moorish style that stood 78 feet over the street. It was the only two-story arcade in the world at the time but struggled to fill all its spaces and ultimately was turned into a parking garage.

Chauncey Hill Mall

Generations of Purdue University students hung out at Chauncey Hill Mall in West Lafayette. It was a three-acre strip mall at the top of the State Street Hill a few blocks from campus, but it was so much more. It had popular hangout spots like Utopia Diner, Parthenon, Jake's Roadhouse, Quincy's Tavern, Wabash Yacht Club, and Garcia's Pizza, a favorite with punks and skaters. It was home to a few arcades and businesses like Pants Explosion, Groucho's Men's Fashions, PJ Woofers, Toogie's Cookies, and Hot Scotch, a fast-food joint specializing in southern fried rabbit. It closed after 40 years in 2018 when developers pursued a more urban redevelopment project. Purdue alumni will not soon forget the 50-cent Den pops at Discount Den.

Courtesy of the Indiana Historical Society

Century Mall

Century Mall at Broadway and US 30 in Merrillville was the little sibling of the nearby Southlake Mall, the second-largest enclosed mall in Indiana. Los Angeles–based Bass Financial developed the Century Mall, which opened in 1979 with the Chicago-based anchors Montgomery Ward and Goldblatt's, which also had nearby locations in Gary and Hammond and which inspired the department store scenes in Region native Jean Shepherd's *A Christmas Story*. The Century Mall had an arcade, a food court, and a few stores, like R-Way and Service Merchandise, but nothing compared to Southlake just down the road. A popular Shakey's Pizza on the edge of the parking lot hosted many kids' birthday parties. It was turned into a discount mall but still declined until it was largely demolished in 2002 after Montgomery Ward went out of business. The site has been partly redeveloped into a strip mall called Century Plaza.

FAIR OAKS MALL

Fair Oaks Mall opened in 1990 in Columbus during the heyday of the shopping mall, when 19 new ones opened around the country. Designed by Cesar Pelli of Gruen Associates, the mall sat on the Bartholomew County Fairgrounds just three miles from the City Center, an indoor shopping mall attached to the Commons civic event space. It survived longer than the Commons Mall that was torn down for redevelopment, but not for much longer. The 413,000-square-foot Fair Oaks Mall offered everyday shopping at stores like Sears, JCPenney, and Dunham's Sporting Goods but declined along with many of its peers in an e-commerce age. The City of Columbus and Columbus Regional Health teamed up to buy it and turn it into a health and recreational campus with a community center, sports courts, exercise areas, a pool, and other amenities promoting holistic well-being.

HOTELS

One of Indiana's greatest preservation stories is how the Cook family saved the West Baden Springs Hotel, a national historic landmark with a 200-foot dome that was once the largest in the world. It was built as a resort at a time when people flocked to the nearby mineral springs, thought to be curative. Just off the Monon Railroad, the "Eighth Wonder of the World" had an opera house, casino, natatorium, and massive atrium with palm trees and birds flying freely. The Chicago Cubs did spring training nearby. Boxers, politicians, and other celebrities flocked to the Disney World of its time. Bloomington's Cook family later spent $30 million of their medical device fortune to save it, but not all of Indiana's historic hotels were so lucky.

Terre Haute House

Courtesy of DPLA via Wikimedia Commons

The historic 10-story Renaissance Revival–style Terre Haute House was razed and replaced with a Hilton Garden Inn that opened in 2007 despite repeated preservation efforts. Its heyday ran from the 1920s to the 1950s, when it was a high-class destination for high rollers who flocked to Terre Haute for its illegal gambling dens. Al Capone and John Dillinger were rumored guests. It opened as the Prairie House in 1838 in the prairie by the future route of the National Road. The four-story hotel had its ups and downs until a new owner razed it to build a much grander structure in 1927. Indianapolis Motor Speedway owner Tony Hulman acquired it in 1959, looking to restore its grandeur. But downtown was in decline as newer hotels opened along the newly constructed Interstate 70 and US 41, eventually putting it out of business.

Red Lantern Inn

The Red Lantern Inn in Beverly Shores was touted as a Miami-like resort on the shore of Lake Michigan. The stone, glass, and cedar hotel on Lake Shore Drive had 25 rooms and a penthouse with sweeping views of the spectacular inland sea and the nearby Chicago skyline. Beckoning the dining public like a lighthouse, it had three large dining rooms, the Ship and the Hold bars, and a banquet hall for 500 that was billed as the largest in Northwest Indiana at the time. Diners watched the waves crash on the rocks below. The National Park Service acquired it in 1971 just five years after the lakefront was transformed into the Indiana Dunes National Lakeshore, which was modeled after the Cape Cod National Lakeshore. It was leased out to a Minnesota-based operator that ran it until 1986, when it closed and was subsequently torn down.

Courtesy of Westchester Township History Museum

Claypool Hotel

Courtesy of IMCPL

The Claypool Hotel in Indianapolis opened at the corner of Illinois and Washington in 1903. It was named after the millionaire Edward Fay Claypool, who bankrolled its construction at the site of the Bates House and, before that, Thomas Carter's Tavern. It was designed by architect Frank Andrews and had the largest lobby in the country at the time. The meeting rooms also were so large it served as headquarters of both the Democratic and Republican parties. It had 460 rooms with brass beds, mahogany dressers, and private baths, an innovation at the time. After two women were murdered there and newer hotels sprang up, it was demolished in 1967. The Embassy Suites Hotel stands there today.

Camp Indiana at Indiana Dunes State Park

Courtesy of the Westchester Township History Museum

The secluded Camp Indiana at the top of Mount Tom at the Indiana Dunes State Park served as a summer retreat for Indiana governors between the 1920s and 1965. They vacationed at the cottage with their families, enjoying the sand and surf of Lake Michigan's South Shore. It stood 150 feet high on the towering sand dune, affording panoramic views of the lake and the state park that was founded in 1925 after an effort by Chicago's Prairie Club to make the Indiana Dunes into a national park. It was a spacious cabin surrounded by pine trees with a screened-in porch with lounge chairs overlooking the beach. The state demolished it after it fell into disrepair so Indiana wouldn't have to continue to fund its upkeep.

Sheraton Hotel

Gary Mayor Richard Hatcher built a new convention center and Holiday Inn in 1967 in the hopes of reviving the downtown. The 14-story, 300-room hotel went up on the site of the long-closed and much more modest three-story Broadway Hotel. Just off the Indiana Toll Road, it had a five-story parking garage and a 165-seat restaurant. But it was so little visited that the top eight floors were closed off in just a few years. Holiday Inn closed shortly after, and it was taken over by Sheraton, which ran it until 1985. An unfinished pedestrian bridge would have connected it to the Genesis Convention Center just across the street, but it trailed off to stairs on the other side of Broadway in a haunting sign of the city's decline.

Courtesy of Gary Lotzman Katzman via Wikimedia Commons

Dunes Arcade Hotel

Courtesy of Westchester Township Public Library

The Dunes Arcade Hotel stood just east of the Indiana Dunes State Park Bathing Pavilion and Restaurant. The restaurant had devolved into a snack shop by the 1930s. The neighboring three-story, 50-room hotel had an Art Deco and Expressionist design that was distinctive and so pretty it ended up on postcards. It was designed by John Lloyd Wright, the son of famed Prairie Style architect Frank Lloyd Wright. Visitors flocked there between May and September from the 1930s to the 1960s. It had an arcade for shopping on the first floor and a large dining room that was open seasonally. After shuttering, it was demolished in 1971.

New Auburn Hotel

Guests have stayed at the New Auburn Hotel at Ninth and Main Streets in Auburn since the 19th century. Construction started in the 1860s on what was originally known as the Swineford House. It housed traveling salesmen in up to 36 rooms. Then, as carriage and automobile factories transformed Auburn's economy, it was renovated in 1919 into the modern Auburn Hotel. While retail businesses lasted for decades on the first floor, the hotel eventually became underutilized, occupied mainly during the Auburn Cord Duesenberg Festival on Labor Day weekend. The hotel was slated for demolition in 2024 after its foundation was deemed unsafe, but the owner who had acquired it because of an interest in historic preservation planned to rebuild it as closely as possible to the original, though it was likely to be converted at least partly into housing.

Courtesy of Eckhart Public Library

CULVER'S GOLDEN RESORT ERA

Courtesy of the Library of Congress

Lake Maxinkuckee in Culver was a major resort area in the late 19th century with attractions like a floating dance hall and Chautauqua, a summer education camp. "Culver and Lake Maxinkuckee were home to several beautiful hotels and other features catering to the booming tourist crowds of the 1880s to the 1910s prior to paving of roads and diminishing of the railroads," Culver Academies Museum's archives manager, Jeff Kenney, said. One of the largest natural lakes in Indiana, Lake Maxinkuckee has long been lined with summer homes ranging from cottages to mansions. Many famous Hoosiers stayed there, including Cole Porter, Booth Tarkington, and Kurt Vonnegut. Tarkington wrote part of *The Gentleman from Indiana* there, and Vonnegut described it as his "Aegean Sea and Eden lost."

Cedar Lake's Golden Resort Era

When the Monon Railroad came to Cedar Lake in 1881, it transformed the sleepy lake town south of Lake Michigan into a major resort area that offered a summer getaway for Chicago. More than 50 hotels sprang up around the shallow, rippling 794-acre lake near the Illinois state line. Hotels like the Sans Souci Hotel, Sigler House, and Cedar Point Hotel sprung up around the shore. They touted amenities like waterslides, rowboats, fishing poles, and even floating music halls. Al Capone allegedly frequented the Kennedy Hotel, which was riddled with bullets allegedly from hit attempts. Some of the hotels had as many as 100 rooms during Cedar Lake's Golden Era in the 1920s. Even the San Damiano Monastery had a hotel. Most of the hotel buildings were razed or repurposed, such as into the Museum at Lassen's Resort.

{MEDIA}

As a seasoned journalist, I've worked in newsrooms in Northern, Central, and Southern Indiana, from the shadow of the rolling hills outside Bloomington to the towering sand dunes along Lake Michigan. After years of running around to city council meetings, house fires, and crime scenes and working with some immensely talented colleagues, I can vouch that Hoosier journalists are a dedicated lot. Indiana has been home to some legendary reporters, broadcasters, and television personalities. Hard-charging Hoosier journalists have won Pulitzer Prizes and countless other awards while chasing deadlines in pursuit of the truth. The state has spawned some legendary journalists, like Ernie Pyle, Theodore Dreiser, Jane Pauley, Steve Inskeep, Asma Khalid, Bill Nangle, Nancy Comiskey, Tim Evans, Eric Deggans, Ida Husted Harper, Bob Hammel, Craig Klugman, Frank Reynolds, Matthew Tully, Bill Dolan, and Bob Zaltsberg. The great sportswriter, playwright, and wit Ring Lardner cut his teeth at the *South Bend Tribune*. Gary native Walt Bogdanich won two Pulitzer Prizes doing investigative reporting for *The New York Times*. "Aesop of Indiana" George Ade, a popular *Chicago Daily News* columnist who was syndicated nationally, is half the namesake of Purdue University's Ross-Ade Stadium, perhaps the only football stadium named after a writer. The Hoosier State has put out some great newspapers, not all of which have survived the tumultuous upheaval as the media industry transitions to the digital age.

Sammy Terry
Courtesy of IMCPL

Courtesy of harlowchickenlooper.com

"The Truth Quick"
The GARY AMERICAN
INDIANA'S GREATEST COLORED NEWSPAPER
PASS ANTI-LYNCHING BILL
Law Will Punish Southern Pastime
NEGRO POLICE ARE SWORN IN IN LOUISVILLE
CRIME TO BE PUNISHED IN DIXIE STATE
GARY AMERICAN BELIEVES ITS OWN IS ENTIRELY NEW NEWSPAPER
LIFE SIREN TO GIRL SLAYER
No Tricks
ADVERTISE

Courtesy of the Library of Congress

Courtesy of Tom Lounges

TELEVISION

Indiana has multiple television markets, including Indianapolis, Fort Wayne, Evansville, South Bend, Lafayette, and Terre Haute. It's also served by the out-of-state Chicago, Cincinnati, and Louisville markets since Indiana is home to suburbs of those neighboring cities. Indiana television stations have produced some notable shows, like *Commander KC* and *Peggy's 59er Diner.* Bob Ross filmed *The Joy of Painting* in a Muncie studio one can visit today on the Minnetrista campus. Indiana also has produced many notable television stars, such as anchor Jane Pauley, actor Greg Kinnear, *The Wire*'s Isiah Whitlock Jr., and Jean Shepherd, who hosted the nationally syndicated *Jean Shepherd's America* that was produced by Boston public television station WGBH.

Courtesy of harlowchickenlooper.com/Freepik

Sammy Terry

Every city has a cheesy horror host who presented late-night B movies on local television stations. Chicago had the rubber-chicken- and-Berwyn-loving Svengoolie; St. Petersburg, Dr. Paul Bearer; Baltimore, Ghost Host; Washington DC, Count Gore de Vol; and Cincinnati, the Cool Ghoul. Indianapolis had Sammy Terry, a play on "cemetery." Bob Carter portrayed the spooktacular ghoul on WTTV and other local stations from the 1960s to the 1980s, emerging from his coffin on Friday nights to trade campy banter with his rubber spider George while showing shlock. His son Mark Carter took over the role in 2010, a few years before his dad died, but appears on television only sporadically, though he's more frequently seen in person at events and online. Like most horror hosts, he sustains a cult following.

Courtesy of Hancock County Historical Society

Cowboy Bob

Cowboy Bob entertained generations of kids on WTTV in Indianapolis, where he hosted the afternoon cartoon show known as *Chuck Wagon Theatre* and later *Cowboy Bob's Corral*. Bob Glaze, a folk singer who donned the folksy television persona, aspired to be a surrogate brother and father to the kids. He worked on the floor crew at Channel 4, recorded an album with a cartoon show host, and landed a TV host job of his own, introducing cartoons from 1970 to 1989. He was originally from Oklahoma and made that part of his act after he took over the *Lunch Time Theater* show. The variety show featured characters like horses, dogs, and Sourdough the Singing Biscuit. He educated kids on animals, fire safety, and other subjects. He went on to produce other programs, like *Indiana Outdoors*, and host *Cowboy Bob's Cable Stable*.

Courtesy of Hancock County Historical Society

Janie

Janie Woods Hodge, long known simply as Janie, hosted the kids' show *Popeye and Janie* that was later known as *Janie* on WTTV in Indianapolis. The teacher and performer, who graduated from the Indiana University School of Music, hosted the cartoon show on Channel 4 from 1963 to 1986. The Indiana Broadcast Hall of Fame inductee sang, danced, played the ukulele, gave kids safety tips, and hosted Girl Scouts and Boy Scouts on the "Janie's Tree House" segment. There was a two-year waiting list to sit on screen and swap jokes with her. She greeted viewers with "Hey, boys and girls" before interacting with puppets like Silly Snake and Gilroy Gopher, hosting animals from the Indianapolis Zoo, and introducing cartoons, often but not always *Popeye*. The show eventually was cut as a result of increased competition from cable.

Don Davis of Don's Guns

Don Davis didn't want to make money, folks. He just loved to sell guns. The white-haired and goateed Davis, looking like an RC Cola version of Colonel Sanders, delivered that line in a billion ads on Indianapolis television stations over the years. It's as burned into people's brains as the car dealer Bob Rohrman pronouncing his surname with a lion's roar or Indiana Beach's earworm "There's more than corn in Indiana" jingle. Davis started selling guns out of a garage in the 1970s when the army veteran was earning a living as a bouncer. He opened Don's Guns and Galleries on Indianapolis's west side, which became one of the top gun retailers in the country by sales volume. It also was repeatedly cited by law enforcement for selling guns later used in crimes. He died in 2016, and his gun emporium closed.

Harlow Hickenlooper

Harlow Hickenlooper hosted the *Three Stooges Show* on Channel 6 in Indianapolis, appeared in a Three Stooges movie, and hosted other television shows. Born Harold Boyton Fryar, he adopted the Harlow Hickenlooper persona of a down-on-his-luck character in a battered straw hat and striped coat for whom things never went right. Cohosting the show with Curley Myers and Captain Star, he did slapstick comedy, sang songs, and often ended skits with a cream pie in the face in front of a studio audience of children. The Indiana Broadcast Hall of Fame inductee played the role of Johnny Ringo on the big screen in *The Outlaws Is Coming* after years of aping the Stooges on the small screen.

Courtesy of Harlowchickenlooper.com

PRINT

Countless newspaper journalists in Indiana cut their teeth chasing deadlines for the *Indiana Daily Student* in the hallowed Ernie Pyle Hall. In 2013, IU's journalism school was folded into a newly created Media School that also encompassed telecommunications and communications and culture. It reflected the decline in print media that's been taking place since home internet service first became mainstream in the 1990s. The state still has many quality newspapers, like the *Indianapolis Star, Times of Northwest Indiana, Gary Post-Tribune, Fort Wayne Journal Gazette, South Bend Tribune*, and *Evansville Courier Journal*. It also has many smaller publications, such as free entertainment weeklies, Spanish-language newspapers, and even a Macedonian publication. Hardworking reporters grind away to keep people informed every single day.

Nuvo Print Edition

When I lived in Indianapolis, an ex-girlfriend marveled at how I always knew whatever cool stuff was going on in the Circle City. I didn't possess any arcane knowledge, just grabbed a copy of *Nuvo* every week. The alt weekly was founded in 1990 in the tradition of *The Village Voice*, *Chicago Reader*, and Seattle's *The Stranger*. Geared toward younger readers, it was filled with coverage of art, music, nightlife, and politics. It told you what was going on in Fountain Square, Mass Ave, Broad Ripple, and other trendy spots around town. It was home to some lively writing, including from the great columnist Steve Hammer, who observed that you could tell whether a neighborhood was well-to-do or struggling based on whether it had AutoZones or auto repair shops. *Nuvo* lives on online but is no longer in print and certainly not on every street corner the way it was.

Courtesy of IMCPL

Fort Wayne News-Sentinel

The News-Sentinel

QUALITY

P. B. Ansell Co.

Courtesy of newspapers.com

Fort Wayne used to be a two-newspaper town. The *Journal Gazette* was the morning paper, and the *News-Sentinel* the evening paper. The *News-Sentinel* was an acclaimed daily, winning a Pulitzer Prize in 1982 for flood coverage. The publication started out as the weekly *Sentinel* in 1833 and merged with the *Fort Wayne Daily News* in 1918. It had a joint operating agreement with the *Journal Gazette* in which each was separately managed editorially but shared the same advertising, circulation, and printing infrastructure. It was long the bigger of the two but was eventually surpassed by its rival as evening papers fell out of fashion. The paper was long run by Helene Foellinger, who started out as the youngest publisher in the country, grew the circulation, and eventually sold to Knight Ridder in 1980. It stopped putting out a print paper in 2017 and laid off its last employee in 2020.

Indianapolis Times

The *Indianapolis Times* won a Pulitzer Prize for its campaign against the Ku Klux Klan in 1928. The evening paper started out in 1888 as the *Indianapolis Sun*, which was billed as "the only one center paper in Indiana." The owners changed the name to the *Evening Sun*, the *Indiana Daily Times*, and finally the *Indianapolis Times* in 1922. It was acquired by Scripps-Howard and managed by Roy W. Howard. It was a crusading paper that tackled subjects like scandals, fraud, corruption, and—most notably—Ku Klux Klan involvement in state politics and Indiana Grand Dragon D. C. Stephenson's relationship to Gov. Ed Jackson. It championed many causes, like supplying kids with winter coats during the Great Depression and running free employment ads during recessions to help out-of-work Hoosiers. It reached a circulation of more than 100,000 on Sundays but ceased publication in 1965.

The Indianapolis Times

No Secret Order Shall Rule Indiana!

FOUR SHOT IN NILES KU-KLUX KLAN RIOT

Former Governor McCray Made Editor of Atlanta Federal Prison Magazine

Courtesy of Wikimedia Commons

Night Rock News

Courtesy of Ken Zurek

Music journalist and record store owner Tom Lounges recalls riding his bike from Highland to Calumet City just across the border in Illinois to grab albums like Kiss's *Destroyer*, which he brought home to play again and again. He later worked at Hegewisch Records, editing its *Night Rock* News newspaper that was widely distributed around Northwest Indiana. He covered acts like Quiet Riot, the Oak Ridge Boys, and Jason Bonham, interviewing so many touring musicians and celebrities that he would later look back through old archives, forgetting he had interviewed Jane Fonda or the Chicago Seven's Tom Hayden. The newspaper chronicled Northwest Indiana's rock scene during a golden era of live music at local venues. "There were five clubs in every town, and all would have a great band playing on a Tuesday or Wednesday," Lounges said. "You could go somewhere like the Midway Ballroom, and it would be standing room only."

Midwest Beat Magazine

Courtesy of Tom Lounges

Midwest Beat Magazine had the scoop on the Calumet Region's music scene. It was originally named *Illiana Beat Magazine* and then *Beat Magazine* before it was changed to Midwest Beat after a trademark dispute. It was published by the mustachioed music scenester Tom Lounges, a radio personality, DJ, booker, and music journalist who wrote for national magazines like *Goldmine* and *Video Rock Stars*. Lounges first published a piece defending Elvis in the *Hammond Times* and covered acts like Jefferson Starship, Grand Funk Railroad, and Joan Jett. He published the *Midwest Beat* by hand, laying out columns on a drafting board himself early on. The publication included features and profiles of touring bands and local acts, letting people know what rock shows were coming up at venues like the Star Plaza in Merrillville or Club Dimensions in Highland. Its writers went on to work in Chicago radio and for the BBC.

Hot Potato

Hot Potato was Indianapolis's first free music magazine. It later expanded to Bloomington and helped young people across the state discover new bands, including underground, alternative, and college rock acts. Founded in 1979, the pioneering free entertainment magazine was followed by publications like *Hijinx*, *Steppin' Out*, *The New Times*, and *Nuvo*. It was started by musician Terry Lowe, who discovered the *Sweet Potato* alternative weekly when playing a gig at a Minneapolis dive bar. Indianapolis had nothing like it at the time, and Lowe was frustrated with the lack of promotion of local acts. Free music publications started springing up across the Midwest, like *Prairie Sun* in the Quad Cities. *Midwest Beat* publisher Tom Lounges in Northwest Indiana recalls that the music magazines would share articles and sometimes even send delegations of bands to play clubs in each other's markets, including the Cleveland-based metal band Mushroomhead before it got big.

Indianapolis News

The *Indianapolis News* was known as the Great Hoosier Daily during its 130-year run. The evening newspaper was founded in 1869, was long run by the Pulliam family, and had the largest circulation in the state before losing readership to the morning *Indianapolis Star*. It published the work of Kin Hubbard, the humorist whose *Abe Martin* cartoon was nationally syndicated and who also wrote the weekly "Short Furrows" humor column. The gag-a-day comic featured the elderly, bearded Abe Martin, a folksy Brown County resident forever cracking wise. The *News* also published the work of novelist and society editor Grace Alexander and "Country Contributor" columnist Juliet V. Strauss, who persuaded the state to establish Turkey Run State Park. The *News* ceased publication in 1999.

THE INDIANAPOLIS NEWS

HOME EDITION

Food Stores to Ignore New OPS Boosts

Charge Lever to Extend Federal Price Controls

Kentucky Convict Is Indicted for Murder of Nurse

Red Army in Korea Now Million

DRIVER NAPS, GOES PLACES

State to Seek Custody of Green Death Suspect

We're Brave

Pole-Car Diesel Stirs Rival's Ire

Liquor Sale Off 40%; One Brand Reduces Price

Rain Throws Chill Into State

Truman Blasts Germ War Lies

Daily Prayer

Dionne Quintuplets, 18 Today, Get Diplomas

LONG-DISTANCE NUDITY IS O.K.

Late Flash

Courtesy of newspapers.com

Indianapolis Leader

Indianapolis's first Black newspaper was the *Indianapolis Leader*. It debuted in 1879, when there were only 30 newspapers for African Americans nationwide. Founders Robert Bagby, Benjamin D. Bagby, and James D. Bagby were the sons of enslaved people. They learned tanning from their parents' former master and relocated to an ex-slave community in Oxford, Ohio. They went to Indianapolis to become principals of all-Black public schools after graduating from Oberlin College. The professional educators decided to put out a four-page weekly newspaper that published society news for the city's Black community. They sold the publication in 1885 when Robert Bagby became the first African American to serve on the Indianapolis City Council. It went on to become a Greenback Party and Union Labor paper under different ownership. It folded in 1891.

THE INDIANAPOLIS LEADER.

Courtesy of Readex via Wikimedia Commons

The Village Sampler

Vol. I, No. 1 — Serving the Broad Ripple Village Community — June, 1987

150

Broad - Ripple - Village

1837-1987

Courtesy of Wikimedia Commons

Village Sampler

Now known as a nightlife district where bros go barhopping, Broad Ripple Village at the bend of the White River on the northeast side of Indianapolis was long known as a bohemian hippie enclave. Named after a phrase coined by Hoosier Poet James Whitcomb Riley, the neighborhood had its own newspaper, the *Village Sampler*. Lillian Rose Barcio, a Butler University publications assistant who took advantage of her free tuition as an employee to earn a journalism degree at the age of 50, started putting out the monthly paper in 1987. Published out of her basement, it put out many articles about the history of Indianapolis and Broad Ripple in particular. It ceased publication in 1998, after Barcio's health declined. But the archives live on at the Indianapolis Public Library.

Be Worthy Of First Class Citizenship

Join The N.A.A.C.P.

The Gary American

VOL NO 40 NO 28 — Oldest Negro Weekly In Northern Indiana

JULY 14, 1967 — 10¢ A COPY

HATCHER DEMANDS ELIMINATION OF DISCRIMINATION AS K'S EQUAL NEGRO '68 SEATING

Governor Richard Hughes
Chairman Special Equal
Rights Committee
1730 K N W
Washington, D. C.

Crucial that your committee immediately adopt rules to eliminate racial discrimination from Democratic Party. Stop Just outlawing segregated delegation not enough-- only if integrated is seated, instead will 1964 promises be honestly kept. Stop 1964 compromise certainly not adequate for 1968.

Richard G Hatcher
Councilman at Large
Gary, Indiana

CLAY RECEIVES NATIONAL SALES ACHIEVEMENT AWARD

CLAY

At a recently held banquet at Sam Remos the Calumet ... the National Sales Achievement Award for successful sales and service in public interest. Other recipients of this award were: Paul Eley, Mutual of New York; Eugene Hicks, Connecticut General, Rich Braman, Massachusetts Mutual and J Lemere.

Clay is also a member of the 1967 Mid America Round Table and was awarded a Silver cup at the Mid America Business Conference held in Miami

LIFE MEMBERSHIP FIGHT FOR FREEDOM DINNER GROSS OVER $16,000

Courtesy of Gary Public Library

Gary American

The *Gary American* served one of the largest Black communities in the Hoosier State from 1927 to the 1990s. Initially published by the Whitlock family, the weekly newspaper was originally known as the *Gary Colored American* but had shortened its name to the *Gary American* by 1928. It covered local news like labor strife at local steel mills and the Steel City's racial integration, such as the Emerson School Walkout that led white students and parents to protest the integration of six African American students. It reported on stories like the city adopting the country's first fair employment practices ordinance, Gary's first Black taxi driver, and the longtime struggle to integrate the Lake Michigan beach at Marquette Park. It covered the civil rights movement, lynchings nationwide, and the local boycott against Kroger for refusing to hire Black workers. It eventually expanded into neighboring East Chicago.

Kokomo Perspective

The *Kokomo Perspective* competed with the daily *Kokomo Tribune* for more than three decades in the blue-collar town of Kokomo, an auto manufacturing hub in Howard County. The free broadsheet was delivered weekly to more than 30,000 households from 1989 to 2021, via the mail for the last few years. It published political, crime, and court news, as well as public records. Online, it was an aggregator that often posted stories from other Indiana papers. Publisher Don Wilson founded the publication and sold it to Brian Oaks, who closed both it and the *Kokomo Herald*. The publication struggled during the COVID pandemic when a lot of its small-business advertisers could no longer afford ads, killing its main source of revenue.

Courtesy of Howard County Public Library

kokomo perspective.com

January 29, 2020

Study commissioned by Goodnight indicates police shortage

Consulting firm found department needed at least five more patrol officers

Republican county council at-large race now contested

Local farmer Daryl Maple joins race

ROBBERIES, DRUGS, GUNS, AND TEEN DEATHS

Area's last three shooting deaths involve teen victims

Salute to FCA US coming

BURN CALORIES. BUILD COMMUNITY.

JOIN TODAY • 765.457.4447 • 114 N. UNION STREET • KOKOMO, INDIANA

La Porte Herald-Argus

War correspondent Ernie Pyle was celebrated as the "voice of the American soldier in World War II." He grew up on an 80-acre farm in Dana, studied at Indiana University, and edited the *Indiana Daily Student*. He left college early to become a reporter for the *La Porte Herald-Argus* before becoming an aviation columnist at Scripps-Howard's *Washington Daily News*. He became beloved because of his depictions of the common soldier's everyday experiences on the front lines. The *Herald-Argus*, where he cut his teeth, covered some unusual stories over the years, such as a rocket slamming into a golf course, a 92-year-old society woman who was murdered with a wine bottle in her home, and a ventriloquist pastor who preached at a local church for 25 years with a dummy known as Gospel Pete. In 2020, the paper merged with the *Michigan City News-Dispatch* amid ongoing challenges in the industry.

The Ryder

Courtesy of IDS

Bloomington has had many alt weeklies, like the *Bloomington Voice*, the *Bloomington Independent*, and the *Bloomington Alternative*. The longest running was *The Ryder*, which focused mainly on arts and culture and had its own film series. It debuted on April Fool's Day in 1979, at a time when a half dozen alternative weeklies were circulated in the free-spirited college town. Former IU English major Peter LoPilato honed his chops at the *Bloomington Examiner*, *Fun City*, and other countercultural publications before starting his own newspaper. He also launched the Ryder Film Series to bring art-house and foreign films to town at a time before streaming, DVDs, or even VHS. The publication featured essays, long-form journalism, event previews, and a cultural calendar that let students, faculty, and townies know what there was to do around town. *The Ryder* stopped publication in 2020, but the Ryder Film Series continues to screen movies around town.

{COMMUNITY}

Several Hoosier communities sprang up as company towns around factories. Gary and East Chicago were built around steel mills, Hammond around a slaughterhouse, and Whiting around a refinery that made kerosene before the automobile was even mass produced. The Indiana Manufacturers Association likes to brag that the Hoosier State is the most manufacturing-intensive state in the union. Northwest Indiana is the steel capital, Warsaw the orthopedic capital, Batesville the casket capital, and Elkhart the RV capital. Indianapolis is home to one of the country's largest pharmaceutical companies, Eli Lilly; the Hoosier State also is one of the nation's leading producers of hardwood furniture, electrical equipment, machinery, and mobile homes. Indiana has always been one of the top automotive manufacturers in the country. In the early days of the auto industry, Hoosier automakers like Studebaker, Stutz, Duesenberg, and Auburn made a splash on the national scene. The state has lost many factories, as well as natural resources like the Limberlost Swamp, the Everglades of the North, and the Hoosier Slide, a towering sand dune by Lake Michigan that was hauled away by the railcar. Several historic train stations and many distinguished architectural marvels have faded from the scene. Entire neighborhoods have been lost. Early settlements have been buried under the ever-shifting sand dunes along the shoreline of Lake Michigan. But Hoosiers are a plucky lot who soldier on.

Grassyfork
Courtesy of Morgan County History Center

Cord Automobile
Courtesy of Eckhart Public Library

Colonial Mineral Springs
Courtesy of Morgan County History Centert

Union Station

Baums Bridge
Courtesy of *The Times of Northwest Indiana*

NATURAL WONDERS

Many people who pass through on the highways assume Indiana's landscape to be flat and unvarying. The drive along Interstate 65 between Crown Point and Indianapolis has been described as one of the most boring in the country. But Indiana is filled with natural wonders to explore, including sand dunes that stand hundreds of feet high along the Lake Michigan shoreline in the Indiana Dunes, the brilliant colors of the fall foliage on the wooded hills in Brown County State Park, and the fossil beds of the ancient Devonian limestone at Falls of the Ohio State Park. One can spelunk in caves, behold waterfalls, or take in other natural treasures across Indiana. But some notable natural wonders were lost to history. Swamps were drained, sand dunes flattened, and forests were clear-cut.

Beaver Lake
Courtesy of Chris Light

Everglades of the North

Courtesy of *The Times of Northwest Indiana*

The Grand Kankakee Marsh was known as the Everglades of the North. The vast system of wetlands around the Kankakee River supported a wide array of flora and fauna. It was one of the largest marshes in the United States, spanning 5,300 square miles. But then Congress passed the Swamp Act in 1852, and ditches were built a few years later to drain the marsh to turn it into farmland. The state helped fund the project, which had drained most of the wetlands by 1910. The Kankakee River was then rerouted by dredging it to make it deeper. It was channelized with levees to ship timber to Illinois sawmills. Only about 30,000 acres of the Grand Kankakee Marsh remain today, but it was immortalized in the PBS documentary *Everglades of the North.*

Limberlost Swamp

Gene Stratton-Porter immortalized the Limberlost Swamp in her novels, most notably *A Girl of the Limberlost.* The 13,000-acre wetland stretched across Adams and Jay Counties in Northeast Indiana, supporting an array of biodiversity and hosting many migratory birds. Legend has it, the swamp was named after "Limber" Jim Miller getting lost there while hunting. Stratton-Porter lived on the periphery, often explored it and photographed its flora and fauna, and lobbied unsuccessfully to preserve it. It was drained by a steam-powered dredge for agricultural use in the early 20th century. A fraction of it has been restored by the Indiana Department of Natural Resources, bringing back some of the wildlife, birds, and insects.

Courtesy of Wikimedia Commons

Beaver Lake

Beaver Lake in Newton County was the largest lake entirely within Indiana before it was drained after the Swamp Land Act of 1850. It spanned tens of thousands of acres but was shallow, never exceeding 15 feet in depth. The lake was home to many fish, waterfowl, and birds, including a robust bald eagle population. Criminals, including horse thieves, robbers, and counterfeiters, used to hide out on the remote Bogus Island on the lake. Land speculators drained it and turned it into farmland. The Nature Conservancy acquired it in the late 1990s and restored the land to prairie. It's now part of the Kankakee Sands Nature Preserve, where a trail rings what was the shoreline.

Courtesy of Chris Light

Blake Gardens

Blake Gardens drew visitors to a pastoral landscape in Clay Township by South Bend. The Blake family developed the Venetian gardens in the 1920s. The property at the corner of State Road 933 and Cleveland Road included a lagoon with an island, pier, and concrete bridge. People could swim and boat there. It was so scenic that it was featured on a postcard and opened up to visitors staying at a nearby Howard Johnson's. Ludwig Blake, the artist who created it, died in 1956, and his wife, Suzana, in 1966. It stayed open until 1997, when it was demolished to make way for a hotel despite efforts to preserve it and get it declared a National Historic Landmark.

Courtesy of St. Joseph Public Library

Hoosier Slide

The Hoosier Slide was the tallest sand dune in the Indiana Dunes. Standing more than 200 feet tall, it was billed as Indiana's top tourist attraction in the 19th century. People climbed up to the top to take in the breathtaking view of the Lake Michigan shoreline for miles around. Some wed on the peak. As the nickname suggested, a popular activity was sliding down the massive sand dune. But the Ball Corp. of Muncie strip-mined it, hauling the sand away by train to make its jars. The composition of the "Singing Sands" on that Michigan City beach, so called because it squeaked underfoot, was what gave the jars their distinctive blue hue. They're still commonly found at antique stores, but all that otherwise remains of the Hoosier Slide is a plaque at the nearby Old Lighthouse Museum.

Courtesy of the Michigan City Historical Society

Mnomen

Courtesy of Lorie Shaull

Mnomen, also known as wild rice, was long a staple of the Potawatomi diet along the South Shore of Lake Michigan. It grew in abundance along the St. Joseph River before it was industrialized. Green sprouts as tall as people covered the surfaces of swales. Floating pads of mnomen plants sprung up every spring after seeds that spent the winter in the muck floated to the surface. Mnomen was traditionally harvested with a canoe and sticks in rice swales. It was eaten every day, often with fish, berries, and maple syrup. It largely vanished from the landscape when the swamps were drained. Some wild rice still grows in swales at the Indiana Dunes National Park, and there are efforts to revive it despite challenges like invasive phragmites and hybrid cattails.

Courtesy of the National Weather Service

Pogue's Run

Like Chicago reversing the course of its river, Indianapolis used engineering to redirect an inconvenient waterway. Pogue's Run on downtown's southern edge was named after one of Indy's first settlers, George Pogue, who encamped in a cabin on the creek. The pestilent, mosquito-infested waterway did not fit Alexander Ralston's design for the city, interfering with the Washington, DC–inspired grid design he envisioned. It was the site of the Civil War's so-called Battle of Pogue's Run, which was less a battle than a stunt at a political convention, and later a flood that killed 10. The city deemed it a nuisance and buried it in a sewer in 1915, redirecting it into a double-box culvert in which it flows under downtown. The underground creek has captivated the public imagination, factoring into Ben Winters's novel *Underground Airlines*, John Green's book *Turtles All the Way Down*, and the movie *Twice Under* about a Vietnam veteran tunnel rat out for revenge.

Fairview Park

Courtesy of IMCPL

The Butler University campus was originally a suburban trolley park on the Central Canal in Indianapolis where people flocked to enjoy landscaped green lawns away from the city's hustle and bustle. The 246-acre park on the northwest side was developed by the Indianapolis Street Railway Company run by *Indianapolis Star* publisher John Shaffer to give riders somewhere to visit at the end of the line. A 12-mile electrified line ran to the picturesque, wooded farmland starting in 1890. Fairview Park was a place to picnic, canoe, and enjoy the natural splendor, as well as the diving Arabian horses King and Queen that plunged into a pond, a unique enough spectacle to draw a visit from the son of Chinese Emperor Guangxu. It had man-made attractions like a miniature train, merry-go-round, and electric fountain. Butler took over in 1922 and moved its campus there after outgrowing its space in Irvington.

Circle Park

Monument Circle is the preeminent public space in Indiana, right in the heart of downtown Indianapolis. Long before the *Soldiers and Sailors Monument* sprang up, Circle Park was located at the site. The three-acre public gathering place was originally called Governor's Circle after the never-occupied governor's mansion there was demolished in 1857. It was officially renamed Circle Park that year, but it wasn't much of a park. Livestock grazed there, and neighborhood boys played there, but it was mostly just an open, often muddy field. After years of public complaints, the city added landscaping, sidewalks, benches, and a statue of Governor Oliver P. Morton that was eventually moved to make way for the towering 284-foot-tall Civil War monument that became a symbol of the city and state.

Courtesy of the Library of Congress

Howard County Sycamore Tree

A giant sycamore tree believed to be 1,500 years old once towered over Howard County a few miles west of Kokomo until a storm toppled it in 1916. The massive 21-ton stump, about 12 feet high and 57 feet around, was hauled for two days by a 35-horsepower tractor to Highland Park, where it is displayed as "an artifact of Kokomo's pioneer days" and billed as "the world's largest sycamore stump." It was covered with a shelter in 1938 and then in 1989 was encased in plexiglass under a pavilion that's also home to Old Ben, the world's largest steer. Now a hollow, gnarled stump big enough to fit a dozen people inside, it's believed the sycamore tree once stood 100 feet tall.

Courtesy of Kokomo Howard County Public Library

RAILROADS

Indiana is known as the Crossroads of America, a reference to all the interstate highways that slice through the state. It's also crisscrossed by more than 4,200 miles of track. Indiana has three Class I railroad main lines and 39 Class II and Class III railroads, including short-line rails that move goods from steel mills and other factories. It's served by Amtrak and the oldest interurban railroad still running in the country: the South Shore Line, which runs from South Bend to Chicago. One also can ride tourist rails like the French Lick Scenic Railway, the Whitewater Valley Railroad in Connersville, or trains at the Hoosier Valley Railroad Museum in North Judson. But once-might railroads have gone the way of the steam-powered locomotive. Many of the state's bygone rail lines are now popular trails like the Erie Lackawanna.

Courtesy of Freepik

Monon Railroad

The Monon Railroad was Indiana's railroad. Also known as the Chicago, Indianapolis, and Louisville Railway, it operated almost entirely within the Hoosier State during its run between 1897 and 1971. It operated up to 540 miles of road on 792 miles of track before it was merged by the Louisville and Nashville Railroad in 1971. The Monon ran to several universities, like Purdue, IU, Butler, Wabash College, and DePauw University. It's the namesake of the Monon Bell that goes to the winner of the annual Wabash/DePauw football game. The train tracks are now owned largely by CSX. Sections in Indianapolis, Bloomington, and Lake County are popular trails, and its memory lives on in the Monon Connection Museum.

Courtesy of Mike Schafer

Terre Haute Union Station

Cincinnati architect Samuel Hannaford designed the Terre Haute Union Station at Ninth and Spruce Streets. It was a grand Romanesque building that stood three and a half stories high. Passengers used it to travel around the country for 67 years, with trains running daily to destinations like Chicago, Atlanta, New Orleans, Miami, New York, and St. Louis. Prominent visitors included Benjamin Harrison, Theodore Roosevelt, William Howard Taft, Franklin Roosevelt, Harry S. Truman, and Buffalo Bill. It was torn down in 1960 and replaced by Indiana State University's African American Cultural Center. The Terre Haute Amtrak Station, another local if less grand rail landmark known as the Big Four Depot, met a similar fate when it was torn down in 1986.

Courtesy of Vigo County History Center

Louisville and Nashville Union Depot

The Louisville and Nashville Union Depot long served as Evansville's Union Station, providing passenger rail services from the L&N and other railroads. The limestone train station on Fulton Avenue opened in 1902 and served as a hub of train travel for nearly seven decades. It outlasted Evansville's rival Chicago & Eastern Illinois Depot, which shuttered in 1935. It shipped enlistees off to both World War I and World War II but began to decline when the interstate system and commercial air travel took flight. The last train left the station in 1971. After revitalization plans stalled, the depot came down in 1985.

Courtesy of Evansville Vanderburgh Public Library

Interurban Elkhart County

Elkhart was the second city in the world with an electric interurban railroad. Electrified rail trolleys ferried people around town for more than 35 years. The Citizens' Street Railway Co. launched horse-drawn carts in 1886, running every 20 minutes. It electrified trolley cars in 1889, a risky gamble on new technology that bankrupted the company by 1893, as the trolley cars suffered mechanical issues and quickly became obsolete. The Northern Indiana Railway bought the line in 1905, extending service to all points of the city and from Elkhart to Mishawaka, Goshen, and Bristol. It thrived for years until the Great Depression, when its demise was blamed on not offering freight service or trips to Chicago. It offered 20,000 rides on the last day of service and was replaced by a bus system just two days later. Today, Elkhart has the Interurban Trolley, a bus service paying homage to it.

CARMAKERS

In the heady early days of the automotive industry, Indianapolis could have become Detroit. Indiana made 200 of the 2,200 makes of cars produced in the United States from 1900 to 1920. Companies that made wagons, buggies, bicycles, and even flour mill equipment like Marmon shifted to producing the cars that were taking the country by storm. Communities across the state, like New Castle, Mishawaka, Connersville, and Columbus, all were home to automakers. Many did not last long, making only a few models before folding or getting bought out. Most, like Kokomo's Haynes Automobile Company, ran out of gas during the Great Depression. Indiana, however, remains a major automotive manufacturing hub. Honda, Subaru, Toyota, and GM all have auto factories in the Hoosier State.

Studebaker

Studebaker was one of the country's largest automakers in the 20th century before reaching the end of the road in 1966. The Studebaker family immigrated from Germany and made a fortune in wagon-making, transitioning to the newfangled automobiles early on. It made cars in South Bend, where it created an outdoor proving ground with 5,000 pine trees planted to spell Studebaker from overhead. Studebaker made 180,000 cars a year with 23,000 employees at three plants totaling 7.5 million square feet spread across 225 acres. It made the Rockne, Champion, Lark, Starlighter, and Avanti, as well as trucks during World War II. Studebaker merged with Packard to try to keep up with Detroit's Big Three but suffered from declining sales. The last vehicle rolled off the line a day after Christmas in 1963. It was the largest employer in South Bend, which suffered economic devastation.

Stutz

The short-lived Stutz Motor Car Company produced some iconic vehicles, like the Bearcat, Monte Carlo, and Model M LeBaron. Stutz had a good run in Indianapolis from 1911 to 1935. Harry C. Stutz founded the company after building the Bear Cat race car for the Indianapolis 500 in under five weeks. It placed 11th and got the nickname "the car that made good in a day." Stutz's race team went on to win national championships, and Stutz placed second in the famed 24 Hours of Le Mans race. The automaker made America's first sports cars and other speedy and luxury cars. The brand was revived with a line of modern retro-look cars from 1968 to 1995. Stutz's long-abandoned factory in downtown Indianapolis was eventually transformed into a haven of arts galleries. It's now also home to froufrou brunch places, artisan coffee roasteries, shops, and an auto museum.

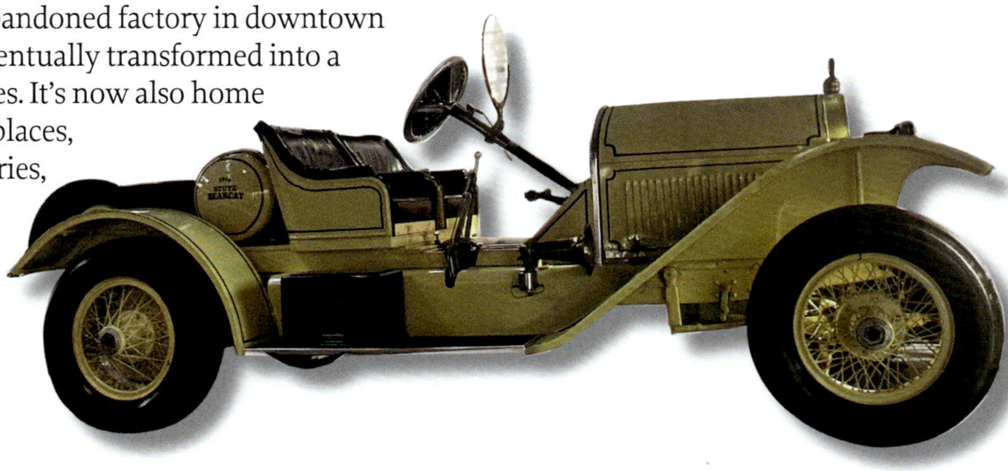

Auburn

Auburn was a high-end car brand eventually wiped out by the Great Depression. It made fast luxury cars under the Auburn, Duesenberg, and Cord marques between 1900 and 1937. Like many automakers, it evolved from a carriage manufacturer—the Eckhart Carriage Company that started in Auburn in 1874. Its flagship vehicle was the Speedster, and it advertised its cars as being supercharged with 150 horsepower and "100 miles per hour or more certified." Its highly stylized cars like the Roadster were too expensive for consumers during the Great Depression, so it switched to kitchen cabinets, sinks, and appliances and later made Jeep bodies during World War II after getting out of the auto business altogether.

Duesenberg

Duesenberg in Indianapolis designed the first American car to win the French Grand Prix. The racing and luxury carmaker dominated the Indianapolis 500 in the early years, winning in 1922, 1924, 1925, and 1927. Brothers Fred and August Duesenberg started out in bicycle racing, soon started designing engines, and designed their first car in 1906. They started Duesenberg Motors Company in Saint Paul, Minnesota, in 1913 and placed 10th in the Indianapolis 500 the following year with the famed pilot and racer Eddie Rickenbacker behind the wheel. They moved the company to Indianapolis in 1920, making more race cars and the commercially produced Model A, which pioneered having hydraulic brakes on all its wheels. Its cars were luxurious, driven by movie stars like Clark Gable and Gary Cooper, and likened to Rolls-Royce. But the company changed hands several times and went out of business in 1937.

Marmon

The Marmon Motor Car Company made luxury cars in Indianapolis in the early 20th century. Howard Carpenter Marmon founded the automaker in 1902, when it started making experimental cars with increasingly powerful engines. It was a pioneering company that invented the rearview mirror, the V16 engine, and the use of aluminum in car designs. It was best known for its Marmon Wasp that driver Ray Harroun drove when winning the first Indianapolis 500 in 1911 after coming out of retirement for just one more race. Marmon produced upscale cars that were popular with movie stars like Douglas Fairbanks and that were fast but reliable like the Model 48, which had limousine options, and the Model 34 that was driven coast-to-coast as a publicity stunt. Despite innovating during the heady early days of the auto industry, Marmon reached the end of the road in 1933 during the Great Depression.

INDUSTRIAL

Indiana is home to more than 8,000 manufacturers that employ over half a million people. It's home to the largest steel industry in the country. Massive steel mills rose up along the South Shore of Lake Michigan around the dawn of the 20th century due to proximity to Chicago's workforce, railroads that could ship steel to customers, and the availability of large tracts of cheap, swampy land near the lake, which allowed iron ore to be transported from Michigan and Minnesota's Iron Range. Immigrants from around the world flocked to Gary, East Chicago, and other Calumet Region cities to make the metal that raised skyscrapers, framed cars, and formed appliances. Manufacturing now accounts for more than a quarter of the state's economic output. But the state is still littered with mothballed factories, idled plants, and shuttered shipyards. Many assembly lines have wound down over the years.

Ball Manufacturoing
Courtesy of Minnetrista

Ball Brothers Glass Manufacturing

Indiana makes stuff. The Hoosier State has the largest share of the workforce in manufacturing nationwide and many blue-collar factory towns like Anderson, Elkhart, Kokomo, Terre Haute, and Muncie, which was such a typical American city that documentarians dubbed it "Middletown." For more than a century, the Ball Brothers Glass Manufacturing Company in Muncie made its famous Ball jars. It produced 60 million canning jars a year by 1905, which people used to preserve fruits and vegetables. It leveled the Hoosier Slide, the state's largest sand dune, so its glass-blowing operations could keep up with demand. The company eventually branched out into other areas, like defense, aerospace, and avionics, getting out of the home canning business and moving to suburban Denver in 1998. It left behind a legacy that included Minnetrista and of course Ball State University, whose alumni include David Letterman.

Courtesy of Ball State University Archives

ChaCha

Google casts a long shadow over a graveyard of defunct search engines like AltaVista, Ask Jeeves, and Lycos. Indiana's entry was ChaCha, a human-guided search engine founded by Carmel entrepreneurs Scott Jones and Brad Bostic in 2006. Named after the Chinese word for search, it marshaled an army of 20,000 freelance guides who helped people find answers via a website, app, and texts. ChaCha fielded up to a million questions a day at its peak in the late 2000s. It proved to be a relic of the pre-smartphone era as people would text 242-242 for answers that they were soon able to look up just as quickly themselves on their phones. It started out with investors like Jeff Bezos but shut down in 2016 when it was no longer bringing in enough advertising revenue to cover its debt.

West Race

Courtesy of Wikimedia Commons

The West Race of the St. Joseph River in South Bend was a hub of manufacturing in the city for more than 60 years, starting in the mid-19th century. More than 15 factories clustered along the rapids, which generated the electricity they needed before electrification. Oliver Plows started along that stretch of the river in 1844, followed by Birdsell Clover Hullers in 1864. It soon became lined with factories that used hydropower to run their machinery. The Coquillard Wagon Works, Singer Sewing Machine Manufacturing, the Stephenson Underwear mill, the Indiana & Michigan Electric Power Company, and the Oliver and Bissell Foundry all operated there up until industry dwindled in the 1910s. The site is now home to the Century Center and Island Park.

Empire Quarry

Indiana is known for the limestone that helped build the Pentagon, the National Cathedral, 35 state capitols, the Biltmore Estate, and the Empire State Building. The Empire Quarry provided the 18,630 tons of stone needed to construct New York City's iconic building. The limestone was quarried by stonecutters in south-central Indiana, around Bedford and Bloomington, where it featured prominently in the classic 1979 film *Breaking Away*. The limestone industry declined when glass and metal skyscrapers that followed the pioneering Seagram Building made stone masonry largely obsolete. After more than 200,000 cubic feet was carved out, the Empire Quarry in Bloomington was closed. The empty rectangle fills with rain and groundwater that attracts swimmers and cliff divers who risk injury jumping off the quarry walls, since the depth can be hard to judge. It's private property, and a no trespassing sign warns that "live ammunition is in use."

Courtesy of IDS

Courtesy of Floyd County Historical Society

New Albany Shipyards

New Albany, a town on the mighty Ohio River, was a shipbuilding hub between 1819 and the Civil War. It made many lavish riverboats, like the *Eclipse*, *Baltic*, and *A. L. Shotwell*, producing $12 million worth of boats. New Albany shipbuilders produced as many as 22 riverboats during the 1860 peak. More than 450 skilled craftsmen, laborers, and mechanics worked at the five largest shipyards during the 1850s, building big ships that hauled goods on the Ohio and Mississippi Rivers with lumber harvested from nearby hardwood forests. New Albany had a strategic location on a shipping route between New Orleans and the Falls of the Ohio. Only Pittsburgh's riverfront moved more tonnage at the time. The shipyards supported another 2,000 to 2,500 jobs at suppliers, meaning plenty of work for blacksmiths, foundries, and cabinetmakers. Eventually, the railroads displaced the shipbuilding industry.

New Albany Glass Works

John B. Ford launched a series of business ventures in Southern Indiana, including a flour mill, iron foundry, rolling mill, and fleet of steamboats. He's best known for starting a glassworks that was the first mass-manufacturer of plate glass in the United States and that helped industrialize New Albany. He opened a plant on the New Albany waterfront in 1865, convinced he could leverage his iron-rolling knowledge to make a cheaper plate glass than they produced in Europe. His company failed, but he tried again with a larger plant and installed the first plate-glass window in a tailor shop downtown. His company was later absorbed into one of the country's largest glass manufacturing firms, Libbey-Owens-Ford. New Albany also produced the Star Glass Works, which grew into one of the country's largest glass plants. Tanneries, a hosiery mill, and other factories followed, making New Albany an industrial hub.

Ford's Star Glass Work's – 1866

Courtesy of Floyd County Historical Society

Grassyfork Fisheries

Courtesy of Morgan County History Center

Martinsville was once known as the Goldfish Capital of the World thanks to Grassyfork Fisheries. The company started in Martinsville in 1899 and produced 40 million goldfish a year, operating what it called the world's largest goldfish hatcheries. Eugene Shireman built it on swampy land unsuitable for farming that he inherited shortly after goldfish first arrived from China and were gaining in popularity in the United States. He started with 200 breeding goldfish, selling off the progeny to retailers and expanding the business over time. The plant on 1,100 acres off Old State Road 37, which included several ponds, was so scenic it was featured on postcards. Standley Byrum bought it in the 1940s and sold it to Ozark Fisheries in the 1970s.

C. G. Conn Band Instrument Factory

Indiana State University Sousaphone Section
Courtesy of Wikimedia Commons

The C. G. Conn Co. factory made saxophones and other brass instruments for years in Elkhart, which is known as the RV capital of the world but which also was a major hub for musical instrument manufacturing. Conn, the plant's namesake, developed mouthpieces for musicians while working in a music store. He would go on to build the largest band instrument factory in the world and become the mayor of Elkhart. He developed the first American-made saxophone, the first sousaphone, and other firsts. "C. G. Conn, the factory itself, was really the leader at the forefront of the industry for decades," Elkhart County Historical Museum Curator of Education Patrick McGuire told WSBT. The building was a landmark that fell into disrepair. It was toppled in 2023 to make room for new housing.

Evansville Shipyard

The Evansville Shipyard helped win World War II. The Ohio River town built more than 170 landing ship tanks or LSTs. The shipyard was built on the river between the Mead Johnson Terminal and the Southern Indiana Gas and Electric Company. It drew thousands of workers to the city. The US Navy watched closely for espionage, fearing the possibility of sabotage, nearly shutting down the landmark Reitz Hill because of its vantage point overlooking downtown. The shipyard was open only from 1942 to 1946, when it burned down, but it made a tremendous impact on the war. People can still tour an LST on the river today. The city has maintained a long tradition serving as a military supplier, for instance making Meals Ready to Eat (MREs).

Courtesy of Evansville Vanderburgh Public Library

GM

Anderson was once home to 20 GM plants. The late-19th-century gas boom brought industry to the city, and factories sprang up around "Pittsburgh on the White River." It became a major auto manufacturing hub when GM built plants there in the 1940s and 1950s, some as big as two million square feet. It employed more than 25,000 workers at the peak. The auto industry started to fade in the late 1970s. Thousands of workers got laid off. Not a single GM plant remains. The city of 60,000 had to tear down more than a dozen of the auto factories to clear the way for new development. Some have been repurposed, while others still sit vacant. The city has since diversified its economy by bringing in health-care jobs, distribution centers, and a racino.

Courtesy of the Library of Congress

Bendix

Courtesy of St. Joseph County Public Library

Bendix, a brand name that was used on washing machines and featured in Archie Comics, got its start in South Bend in 1924. It made a variety of products for cars, planes, radios, televisions, and computers. It produced everything from electric power systems to brake shoes for General Motors and other automakers. It constantly engineered new products, like an electronic fuel injection system for Chrysler, the first computerized antilock brakes, and telemetry components for surface-to-air missiles and the ground stations for the first crewed space flights. Another South Bend company, Bendix Home Appliances, made washing machines while licensing its name. It was in fact the first company to bring a domestic washing machine to market and had sold more than two million units by 1950. Bendix was later sold to Honeywell, and much of the manufacturing campus on South Bend's west side was torn down in 2022.

Hummer

South Bend-based AM General long produced two iconic vehicles: the Humvee used by the army and the civilian Hummer that was modeled on it. The company's Mishawaka factory started making the diesel-powered Humvee trucks in 1985, and they went on to be used in the Cold War, the Somali Civil War, and the wars in Iraq and Afghanistan. The company made more than 280,000 of the light troop trucks that replaced Jeeps and were in turn replaced with MRAPs and Joint Light Tactical Vehicles due to a lack of armor that made them vulnerable to roadside bombs. It made the four-wheel-drive civilian Hummer from 1992 to 2006. Arnold Schwarzenegger helped popularize the humongous militaristic vehicles that were disparaged by some as gas guzzlers and symbols of excess.

Courtesy of Wikimedia Commons

HOSPITALS AND HEALTH CARE

Visitors can view more than 15,000 artifacts at the Indiana Medical History Museum in Indianapolis, including iron lungs, brain specimens, and full skeletons. The former Central State Hospital has the oldest surviving pathology facility in the country. The museum also includes the former medical school amphitheater, an autopsy room, an anatomical exhibit, and laboratories that focused on bacteriology, clinical chemistry, and histology. Visitors can tour an intact re-creation of a small-town doctor's office or stroll through a medicinal plant garden where herbal remedies were cultivated. Listed on the National Register of Historic Places, the museum allows visitors to walk through the history of medicine as it evolved in the Hoosier State. It gives a peek into health care's past in Indiana.

Courtesy of Freepik

Indiana State Sanatorium

The Indiana State Sanatorium opened in 1907 in Rockville. It functioned as Indiana's main hospital for tuberculosis from 1908 to 1968, doing triple duty as a mental hospital and a nursing home. It reopened in 1976 as the Lee Alan Bryant Health Care Center, which served as a private nursing home and mental hospital for a few more decades. It abruptly closed in 2011. All patients were transferred, but most of the medical equipment and hundreds of beds were left behind. Today the abandoned 120,000-square-foot hospital and the supporting buildings sprawling across a 200-acre site have become a popular destination for urban exploration and paranormal investigation.

Courtesy of Indiana Historical Society

Central State Hospital

Courtesy of IMCPL

In the 19th century, people used to take streetcars on leisurely weekends to Central State Hospital in Indianapolis to picnic and watch the mentally ill. It was originally known as the Central Indiana Hospital for the Insane. Indiana state lawmakers voted to establish an insane asylum in 1827, but it didn't open until 1848. It was meant to serve patients across the state, but other psychiatric hospitals opened around the state, so it narrowed its focus to Central Indiana. The campus, whose most architecturally ornate building was known as the Seven Steeples, housed as many as 2,500 patients in 1950. It closed in 1994 due to a variety of factors, including abuse, lack of funding, and more enlightened methods of psychiatric treatment. The campus's pathology building is now the Indiana Medical History Museum, which offers tours.

St. Francis Beech Grove

Countless people were born, died, and were treated at St. Francis Hospital in Beech Grove. The 12-story hospital long powered the economy of the small "city within a city" of Beech Grove that's entirely encircled by Indianapolis. The towering hospital, the largest building in town, encompassed nearly 900,000 square feet. Mishawaka-based Franciscan Alliance decided to shutter the hospital and relocate the services to the newer Franciscan Health Hospital campus just north of County Line Road about seven miles south. Beech Grove took the loss hard. One resident told WFYI that they "had their babies at St. Francis. It was basically cradle to grave. It's like seeing a friend pass on." It closed in 2021 and was later demolished after several redevelopment plans fell through.

Courtesy of IMCPL

Franciscan Health Hammond

St. Margaret Hospital started in 1898 when nuns took a train to Hammond to turn an old farmhouse in the fledgling city, then a company town known as State Line Slaughterhouse, into a hospital. Doctors there treated their first patient while carpenters were still hammering nails into the walls. Early operations took place on a kitchen table. It grew into the largest hospital in Lake County with 226 beds, nine stories, and Northwest Indiana's first neonatal intensive care unit, which was copied from a Chicago hospital. But after 124 years, Franciscan Health decided to shut it down after spending more than $570 million to build new hospitals in more affluent suburbs, including at a Munster hospital just six miles away.

Mineral Water Sanitariums

The neon sign on the historic Union Block building on the courthouse square greeting visitors to downtown Martinsville boasts it is the City of Mineral Water. The mineral water sanitariums are long gone but have a rich history. A dozen different sanitariums have operated in the Morgan County town since Barnard opened in 1888. Home Lawn, the last one left standing, closed in 1968. West Baden Springs in French Lick was better known nationally, but Martinsville was a hub of mineral springs retreats between the 1880s and the 1950s, ranking as one of the top three in the country. People flocked to retreats like the Martinsville Sanitarium to seek treatments for various ailments. The mineral water burbled up from artesian wells, giving the high school teams their Artesian nickname.

Martinsville Mineral Springs
Courtesy of Morgan County History Center

SCHOOLS AND CHURCHES

Education has come a long way in Indiana since Joseph Hess built the Little Red Schoolhouse in Hammond's Hessville neighborhood in 1869. The one-room schoolhouse was heated with a potbelly stove and had one teacher teaching every subject over the course of the school day. Today, high schools like Carmel, Center Grove, and Lake Central get compared to college campuses, boasting amenities like radio stations, auto shops, planetariums, and e-sports facilities. Worship in Indiana has similarly evolved from traveling preachers on the frontier to massive megachurches like Family Christian Center in Munster, Northview Church in Carmel, and First Baptist Church in Hammond that ranked among the largest in the country, drawing so many parishioners as to need parking garages in some cases.

Fairmount High School
Courtesy of Marion Public Library

Heavilon Hall

Generations of English students studied at Heavilon Hall at Purdue University before it was demolished in the summer of 2024 when Purdue moved all its language studies into Stanley Coulter Hall. Heavilon Hall had been a major academic building on campus since 1894, when it was built and then destroyed by a fire after a boiler exploded four days after it opened, inspiring the phrase "one brick higher" that Boilermakers still use to this day. It was originally a mechanical engineering building with a locomotive testing plant and was rebuilt almost immediately, reopening a year later. It had a 140-foot tower with a clock and four bells that would chime on the quarter hour. It was rebuilt in 1959 when it became home to the English Department and Purdue University Writing Lab. The clock was later moved to the Mechanical Engineering Building and the bells to the Purdue Bell Tower.

Courtesy of Boston Public Library

Fairmount High School

Before a car crash cut his life short, the dashingly handsome James Dean embodied teen rebellion in classic 1950s films like *Rebel Without a Cause*, *East of Eden*, and *Giant*. But before blazing through a five-year film career that enshrined him as one of the greatest movie stars of all time, the Marion native graduated in 1949 from Fairmount High School, also the alma mater of *Garfield* creator Jim Davis. The three-story red brick and limestone schoolhouse shuttered in 1986. Indiana Landmarks named it one of the state's most endangered landmarks for three straight years in 2001, 2002, and 2003. Plans to restore the building and turn it into a museum, library, and community center never came to fruition. The school collapsed in 2013 when the roof caved in.

Courtesy of Indiana Landmarks

Oscar C. McCulloch School No. 5

Thousands of visitors a year see the rebuilt facade of Oscar C. McCulloch School No. 5 in the Indiana State Museum. The museum at White River State Park displayed the school that served disadvantaged children and immigrants in the Haughville and White River neighborhoods. The school at Washington and Blackford Streets served hundreds of children in a neighborhood that was home to many different ethnicities, including Black, Chinese, Slovenian, Bulgarian, Romanian, Greek, and Lithuanian. It provided immigrants with citizenship, civic, and English language classes. It offered free services like dental care and day care. It was eventually adapted to serve children with mental and emotional challenges as the neighborhood thinned when auto jobs dried up. But there was outrage and lawsuits when the state demolished the school in 1985. So the facade was rebuilt as a building-within-a-building to teach museumgoers about the history of education in Indiana.

Assumption Catholic Church

Assumption Catholic Church was not only the first Catholic place of worship in Evansville but also a grand cathedral-like parish with a towering steeple. The church started in 1836 but outgrew its original space at Second and Sycamore Streets. The congregation bought a lot across from the Old Central School in 1871, and the church was built a year later. A school opened next door in 1881, and it served as the main church when the Diocese of Evansville was established in 1944. But by the 1960s, Evansville looked to tear it down to build a new Civic Center. The Vatican gave approval to sell the property to the city at a time when the downtown was shedding population and was also served by the Holy Trinity and St. Mary's churches. It was torn down in 1965. The site is now occupied by the Winfield K. Denton Federal Building.

Cadle Tabernacle

Courtesy of Boston Public Library

Cadle Tabernacle in Indianapolis was the largest church of its kind, with a seating capacity of 10,000. It broadcast evangelical radio shows to listeners across the Midwest and South via Cincinnati-based radio station WLW. Businessman E. Howard Cadle had converted to Christianity while ridding himself of alcohol and gambling addictions. He built a massive church for $305,000 in 1921 to evangelize after seeing how popular traveling revival tours were. It boasted 1,400 seats for just the choir. More than 10,000 were turned away for the dedication ceremony. It was later turned into a convention center that hosted boxing, dance marathons, a Ku Klux Klan meeting, and a speech by Martin Luther King Jr. It broadcast the radio show *The Nation's Family Prayer Period* in which Cadle talked about how he went from being an alcoholic to finding God.

City Methodist Church

What was once the largest Methodist church in the Midwest now draws comparisons to Chernobyl. The long-abandoned City Methodist Church in Gary is a crumbling cathedral carved out of Bedford limestone in a steel mill town plagued by blight and disinvestment. The nine-story Gothic church was erected in 1925 and drew as many as 3,000 worshipers in its heyday; more recently it has drawn urban explorers from across the globe. It was dubbed "Seaman's folly" by people who thought Pastor William Seaman was being too ambitious. It closed in 1975 because of high maintenance costs when congregants were fleeing to the suburbs. It was damaged in the Great Gary Arson of 1997. The roof later collapsed. It has been featured in films like *A Nightmare on Elm Street* and *Transformers: Dark of the Moon.*

Art-Psychology Building

The Art-Psychology Building on the Valparaiso University campus burned down in 2022. It had served as an incubator for artwork for both students and faculty. The building was developed by students, whose initiative was featured in the movie *Venture of Faith*. Students raised funds, designed, and built a new engineering laboratory building to reinstate a four-year engineering program after World War II. It opened in 1949 with the sign "Initiated by students; planned by students; built by students." It housed Valpo's College of Engineering until 1968, when the art and music departments were moved there after the Kinsey Hall fire in 1970; engineering moved to the Gellersen Engineering and Mathematics Center. The music department later moved out. It hosted many art exhibits over the years, giving students a venue to showcase their work. Some professors lost decades' worth of artwork in the fire.

Courtesy of *The Times of Northwest Indiana*

Theodore Roosevelt High School

Gary's Roosevelt High School has been named one of the most endangered buildings in the country. The high school in Gary's Midtown neighborhood educated African American students during segregation and became a source of pride in the community. One of just three high schools in Indiana that was built exclusively for Black students, it produced many successful graduates, like NBA number one draft pick Glenn "Big Dog" Robinson, gold-medal-winning boxer Charles Adkins, and two-time Olympic track gold-medal winner Lee Calhoun. Built in 1930, the impressive Colonial Revival school spanned 415,000 square feet and more closely resembled a college campus. One of the largest Black high schools in the Midwest, it won many championships before it closed in 2019 when pipes burst during freezing temperatures, causing widespread water damage throughout the building that would have cost millions of dollars to fix. Gary is now looking to redevelop the school.

Culver Main Barrack

The Culver Academies rebuilt a replica of the historic Main Barrack that housed the first students at the military boarding school. The residential building on the north shore of Lake Maxinkuckee featured architectural elements like an eagle emblem and limestone ornamentation. Generations of cadets lived in the building on the perimeter of the Roberts Quadrangle of the college preparatory military boarding school that Henry Harrison Culver founded in Marshall County in 1894. Students receive rigorous education in a strict military setting and do service projects like building the Skyland Camp-Bowman Lake Ranger Station in Glacier National Park in Montana. It has produced many successful graduates in all walks of life, including film critic Gene Siskel, boxer George Foreman, Kansas City Chiefs owner Lamar Hunt, New York Yankees owner George Steinbrenner, and Oscar-winning screenwriter Edmund H. North.

Courtesy of the Library of Congress

FORTS

French fur traders, British soldiers, and US settlers established forts across Indiana dating back to when it was still untamed frontier, long before the Northwest Territory was even established. Some forts were established to protect settlements. Others held strategic positions during the French and Indian War, the Revolutionary War, the Northwest Indian War, and the War of 1812. They were the site of battles like the Siege of Fort Sackville and the Battle of Tippecanoe. Several forts, for instance, were constructed in Vincennes to defend a key trading outpost on the Wabash River. No battle has taken place in Indiana since the Civil War's Battle of Corydon unless you count the Battle of Broadway that pits the Andrean and Merrillville high school football teams against each other every fall.

Battle of Tippecanoe
Courtesy of the Library of Congress

Fort Wayne's 1816 Fort

Fort Wayne was an actual fort. The city was strategically located where the St. Joseph and St. Mary's Rivers form the Maumee River, allowing goods to be moved as far as the Gulf of Mexico via rivers with some portage. The French built Fort Miami on the St. Mary's River to protect their fur trade interests. General Mad Anthony Wayne was sent by the US government to establish an outpost in 1873. He overcame Native American resistance on the country's then-northwest frontier during the Battle of Fallen Timbers. He then built a permanent fort at the three rivers in 1794. Three more US government forts would be built in downtown Fort Wayne, including a fort that survived a British siege during the War of 1812, holding the frontier as American territory. The last fort was decommissioned in 1819 and turned into a school for the Miami tribe.

Fort Harrison

Courtesy of the Vigo County History Center

Historians call Fort Harrison in Terre Haute, not to be confused with Fort Benjamin Harrison in Lawrence, the Fort of Two Presidents. General, later territorial governor, and eventual president William Henry Harrison built the Fort Harrison stockade at a strategic location on the banks of the Wabash River in Terre Haute a year before the War of 1812. Harrison encamped his troops there before the Battle of Tippecanoe against an army led by Shawnee prophet Tenskwatawa a month later. The fort protected the then–Indiana Territory capital Vincennes downstream as well as the army's supply lines. Future president Zachary Taylor, then a captain, took command during the War of 1812. He achieved America's first major land victory in the war during the Siege of Fort Harrison later that year despite having only 15 able-bodied soldiers and another five settlers in fighting shape. They defended the fort against a force of 600. The fort was abandoned when the frontier continued westward in 1818.

Le Petit Fort

A Revolutionary War battle took place in Indiana at Le Petit Fort, a French fur-trading depot near the mouth of Dunes Creek where it flows into Lake Michigan at what is today Indiana Dunes State Park. In 1780, Capt. Jean Baptiste Hamelin and Lt. Thomas Brady led 30 militia members from Illinois to plunder Fort St. Joseph in Southwest Michigan, taking furs after traveling there via the Illinois, Kankakee, and St. Joseph Rivers. British commander Lt. Dagreaux Du Quindre rounded up Potawatomi and loyalists and chased them across the Indiana Dunes, where they holed up in the vacant Petit Fort. They were eventually overwhelmed by the British forces, which killed four, wounded two, and captured seven. A few escaped into the woods. The loss is credited with slowing the Americans' efforts to capture Detroit, which was considered the key to controlling the Northwest Territory.

Fort Ouiatenon

Courtesy of Jim Hammer

People flock to a replica of Fort Ouiatenon every year for the Feast of the Hunter's Moon historical reenactment near West Lafayette. The real thing was destroyed by a militia in the Northwest Indian War in 1791. The French military outpost and trading post on the Wabash River was the first fortified European settlement ever built in Indiana, in what was known as New France during the 18th century before it became the Northwest Territory and eventually the 19th state. The palisaded stockade was originally home to a major French settlement of trappers from Quebec. It was taken over by the British during the French and Indian War and then by natives in 1763 who drove out the Brits without firing a shot. President George Washington ordered it to be burned down as local tribes used it to resist westward expansion. A Kentucky militia killed 38 natives carrying out that order.

NOTABLE PLACES

Indiana is a place where indelible memories are made, such as when thundering race cars rocket by at the Indianapolis Motor Speedway, when surveying the oceanic expanse of Lake Michigan atop a towering sand dune, or while taking in the brilliant fall colors of tree canopies in Brown County. Hoosiers can gaze over the landscape in a hot-air balloon high above Conner Prairie, kayak down the Central Canal in downtown Indy, watch the mighty Ohio River flow past, scamper amid the hulking dinosaur skeletons at the Children's Museum of Indianapolis, scuba dive to Lake Michigan shipwrecks, or explore the cavernous sandstone gorges at Turkey Run State Park. Indiana is filled with notable places, but some have been erased as time has marched on.

Horace A. Tuttle
Courtesy of Michigan City Public Library

Horace A. Tuttle Shipwreck

Lake Michigan is filled with shipwrecks from a bygone maritime era, including the *F. W. Wheeler* and the *J. D. Marshall.* The *Horace A. Tuttle* was a massive bulk freighter built in 1887 that stretched 250 feet long and 38.7 feet wide, with a draft of 20 feet. It moved agricultural products across the Great Lakes until it was beset by a storm in late October 1898, around the dreaded annual Gales of November when the inland oceans get choppy and harrowing. It sank in about 24 feet of water off the shore of Michigan City. The entire crew of 14 sailors survived after they were rescued by the local lifesaving station. The cargo of corn was lost in Lake Michigan. Michigan City residents would claim the stench of rotten corn would wash up on the beach for years after the ship sank.

Courtesy of Michigan City Public Library

Tomlinson Hall

Courtesy of IMCPL

Indianapolis druggist Stephen D. Tomlinson's will called for the construction of a public building on East Market Square. The city built a public meeting hall named in his honor at the corner of Market and Delaware Streets in 1886. It stood next to the still-extant Indianapolis City Market but was razed after it suffered damage in a fire in 1958, reportedly after a pigeon dropped a lit cigarette on it. The auditorium sat up to 4,200 people, including for a fundraiser for the construction of the *Soldiers and Sailors Monument* that was attended by William Tecumseh Sherman, a centennial celebration, concerts, conventions, and political shindigs like Benjamin Harrison's nomination party. Crowds flocked there to see John Philip Sousa and Rudolph Valentino. It was deemed a fire trap even before a smoking pigeon may have torched it to the ground. People can explore the basement, now known as the Catacombs, on guided tours with Indiana Landmarks.

Frank C. Ball Mansion

Courtesy of Minnetrista

The Ball Brothers made the iconic canning jars that remain pantry staples today and made major contributions to Ball State University in their home base of Muncie. Frank C. Ball built a landmark mansion in the city on the White River. The grand home had many ornate flourishes, like a stained-glass Tiffany window featuring a peacock. It burned down in 1967, nearly 20 years after the family moved out. More than 50 firefighters battled the blaze all night in 10-degree weather but to no avail. It lives on in the Minnetrista museum that was built on its spot with columns that were salvaged from the mansion.

Courtesy of David Kurvach

Hindostan

The ghost town of Hindostan was named by the British immigrant Caleb Fellows, who served with the East India Company before making his way to the then-frontier of Indiana. It was founded in 1816 on the East Fork of the White River on the stagecoach route between New Albany and Vincennes. It grew quickly, with many settling in houseboats on the river. It became one of the largest communities on the Indiana frontier with more than 1,200 residents and the largest community in Daviess County, where it was the original county seat. Just four years later, an epidemic of disease—possibly cholera or yellow fever—ravaged the community, killing half the population and tanking its economy. It was abandoned by 1853. All that remains is a memorial marker in an Indiana state fishing and recreation area. The town is extinct, but people still come to see the Hindostan Falls on the river.

Snyderman House

The acclaimed architect Michael Graves, a Hoosier native who designed 2,000 products for Target and notable buildings like the Portland Building, the Humana skyscraper in Louisville, and the central branch of the Denver Public Library, designed the Snyderman House in Fort Wayne in 1973 for Sanford and Joy Snyderman. It was widely celebrated by the press as a national landmark of modern architecture. It was deemed "a central work" in his celebrated and sophisticated career that included the NCAA headquarters on the canal in downtown Indy. The house had a cage-like Cubist exterior frame around an undulated terra-cotta facade, gray wall planes, and spare glass. The Snydermans lived there for 25 years but then sold it to developers who wanted to bring in a larger housing development. Preservationist groups fought to save the building. The house fell into disrepair and burned down in a suspected arson in 2002.

Courtesy of Todd Zeiger/Indiana Landmarks

Old Ben

Courtesy of Howard County Public Library

Old Ben in Kokomo was the world's largest steer. He weighed 125 pounds when born in Miami County in 1902 and put on 100 pounds a month. By month 20, Old Ben literally weighed a ton. He weighed two tons within a few years. The steer was paraded around to so many fairs across the state that the Nickel Plate Railroad added a spur to his farm so he would be easier to transport. He was put down in 1910 after breaking his leg, but Kokomo acquired the mount and displayed it in Highland Park. Old Ben became nationally known in World War II when Midwestern soldiers bragged about the world's largest steer and asked the *Kokomo Tribune* to send proof. A photo of a woman standing in front of the steer stretching out her arms was sent to soldiers around the globe.

The Business Men's Association Building

The Business Men's Association Building in Evansville, also known as the Grein Building, was built on the site of the old Assumption Catholic Church in the late 1880s. The five-story Romanesque building was originally home to the Mercantile Commercial Bank and boasted an imposing facade with brownstone masonry, red granite, and an 18-foot arch. The mid-rise office building at Second and Sycamore Street next to the Grand Theater and Vendome Hotel was sold to Ann Grein in 1938 and hosted offices for lawyers and oil companies during the city's short-lived oil boom. It was razed in 1972 to make way for an urban redevelopment project.

Courtesy of Wikimedia Commons

Sedley Bridge

The Sedley Bridge was long known as the Rickety Bridge in the Valparaiso area. The one-lane nine-span timber trestle bridge spanned the Norfolk Southern and CSX railroad tracks near Wheeler in Porter County. Built in 1915, the 201-foot bridge on Sedley Road or County Road 475 West had only a single lane for traffic, so drivers had to wait if someone was already crossing, leading to games of chicken. *The Times of Northwest Indiana* described it as a wooden nightmare that withstood attempts to demolish it for more than 20 years. Drivers from Sedley and other rural outskirts long traversed the wooden-plank bridge to get to shopping and restaurants in nearby Valparaiso. The Rickety Bridge lasted 83 years before it was replaced in 1999 by a new bridge that was the first in Indiana to use precast concrete through-girders.

Courtesy of Chris Light

Felt Buildings

John Felt was a self-taught architect who designed many homes and schools. His portfolio included one of Greenfield's most notable hotels. "The Columbia Hotel, later known as the Riley Hotel, was a beautiful four-story structure that had a limestone facade," Hancock County Historical Society board member Brigette Cook Jones said. "It was built in 1896 and would fall into disrepair by the late 1950s. It would be demolished after a couple of fires weakened the structure." Felt designed the original Greenfield High School that opened in 1895 and taught high schoolers until 1926. It was renamed Riley Elementary, serving as the town's elementary school until 1981. "It was under renovation for senior living apartments when it caught fire and burned in 1985," Jones said. "Only the front arches of the building were able to be salvaged, and today they serve as the entrance to the Greenfield Central Administration building."

Courtesy of Lawrence County Museum of History

Courtesy of Calumet Regional Archives

Spanish Castle

Spaniards who immigrated to the burgeoning steel town of Gary in the early 20th century built a castle. They were the first Spanish speakers in the mill town, arriving long before Mexicans or Puerto Ricans. The Unión Española benevolent society raised the Spanish Castle as a community center at the corner of 11th Street and Van Buren Avenue. During the peak migration period, Gary amassed a Spanish population of around 2,700 people who came for opportunities at the steel mill. More Spaniards settled in neighboring Hammond and East Chicago. The Spanish Castle served as a gathering place that had a soccer team and provided recreation, education, and mutual aid funds. Today, it's been taken over by the 20th Century Missionary Baptist Church but still has recognizable Spanish architecture, including the barrel clay roof tiles.

Courtesy of Wikimedia Commons
https://creativecommons.org/licenses/by-sa/3.0/deed.en

Benham West

Benham West was a bygone African American neighborhood in Elkhart. Often known as the Village, it was located west of Benham Avenue where Martin Luther King Jr. Drive turns into Sixth Street. It was home to the Booker T. Washington Community Center, the South Side School, and Black-owned businesses like Webb's Barbecue, Spotville's, Looties, Les Slayton's gas station, Fox Liquor Store, and the Cozy Corner Tavern. Most of Benham West was leveled for a federal urban renewal project that never came. After changes in the city's administration, promised investments like parks, schools, and homes never materialized. As residents have died off, elders have preserved memories of the neighborhood with an oral history project, book, and the documentary *What Happened at Benham West: African American Stories of Community, Displacement and Hope.*

El Barrio

Indianapolis has a lost barrio that was displaced by an interstate highway. El Barrio was a pocket of Hispanic people and culture. Mexican families settled in an area downtown between North and Market Streets and Pine and Davidson Streets, near where exit 112B off Interstate 65 is now. Many of El Barrio's residents worked at the Indianapolis Union Railway and Zaph's, a nearby Greek restaurant. They shopped at El Nopal Market, one of the city's first Mexican grocers, and worshiped half a mile away at St. Mary of the Immaculate Conception Roman Catholic Church. They gathered in each other's backyards to share food, at the Hispano-American Association Service Center that spawned the *La Voz Latina* radio show on WIAN, and at the Trowel Trades building, where Club de la Amistad brought in Mexican musicians like "Accordion King" Lalo Aguirre. Residents dispersed as Indianapolis bought up land for I-65.

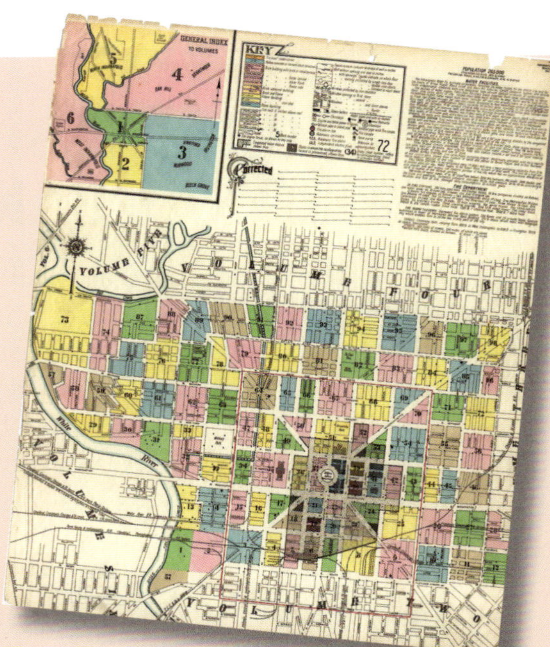

Courtesy of Indiana State Library

Zipper Building

The Zipper Building was long a landmark at the intersection of East Washington and Pennsylvania Streets and Virginia Avenue in downtown Indianapolis. It was one of many flatiron buildings in Indianapolis due to the angled avenues Alexander Ralston had sliced through the city's grid. Originally, the Vance Block featured an Oolitic limestone façade, an 80-foot tower, and the city's first elevator. Indiana Trust took over the grand building that housed professionals like lawyers and architects. The bank found success establishing a trust serving individuals and sought out minority customers, printing savings passbooks in German and employing lobby guards who spoke foreign languages. It merged with Merchants National Bank, which built a new triangle-shaped black-and-white building with trapezoidal windows and a clock in 1960. An architect compared it to whale's teeth or a set of dominos. It was remodeled in 2007 by a realty firm and is no longer recognizable.

Courtesy of the Indiana Historical Society

Courtesy of Bob Hall via Wikimedia Commons

MERCHANTS NATIONAL BANK

Merchants National Bank at Washington and Meridian Streets was the first in Indianapolis to install a safe deposit vault. The bank built the city's first skyscraper of 17 stories in 1913 with a design by famed Chicago architect Daniel Burnham. Now known as the Barnes and Thornburg Building, it stood as the city's tallest structure for a half century until the City-County Building was built in 1962. The bank opened neighborhood branches across the city, including the State Bank of Massachusetts Avenue that John Dillinger robbed. It had grown to 22 branches by 1965, growing its assets to more than $500 million. The bank eventually moved into Merchants Plaza, the site of the Hyatt Regency Hotel at Washington Street and Capitol Plaza downtown. Notably, it put together financing to help lure the Colts from Baltimore, grew by buying 20 banks in four years, and landed a military contract to provide banking to service members abroad. It eventually was purchased by the National City Bank of Cleveland, getting swallowed up like innumerable homegrown banks around the state.

Indiana National Bank

Indiana National Bank was one of the grandest in Indianapolis. A. Bohlen and Son, Architects designed the neoclassical building at 3 Virginia Avenue with an Oolitic limestone exterior and a white Italian marble interior based on banks in New York City in the late 19th century. The fireproof bank building opened in 1897, two years after the bank's last headquarters burned down. Two more stories were added onto the bank in 1912, another two stories in 1935, and six more stories in 1950, along with high-speed elevators and air- conditioning. Indiana National Bank moved into a 37-story skyscraper downtown and sold its architecturally distinguished headquarters to Jefferson National Life Insurance Company in 1967, but it was razed just three years later.

Courtesy of the IMCPL

Greyhound Bus Depot

The Art Moderne Greyhound Bus Station was a distinctive landmark in downtown Fort Wayne. The Streamline bus depot at 223 West Jefferson Boulevard was designed by architect William S. Arrasmith and built in 1938. It was a dramatic blue building with blue Carrera glass, dark blue banding, and a neon sign as a running greyhound. Its sleek horizontal look gave it an aerodynamic feel that suggested the motion of the open road. Similar stations like the one in Evansville have been preserved and repurposed, but it was torn down in 1992. It has since been replaced by Parkview Field, the home of the TinCaps, that often is regarded as one of the finest minor-league ballparks in the country.

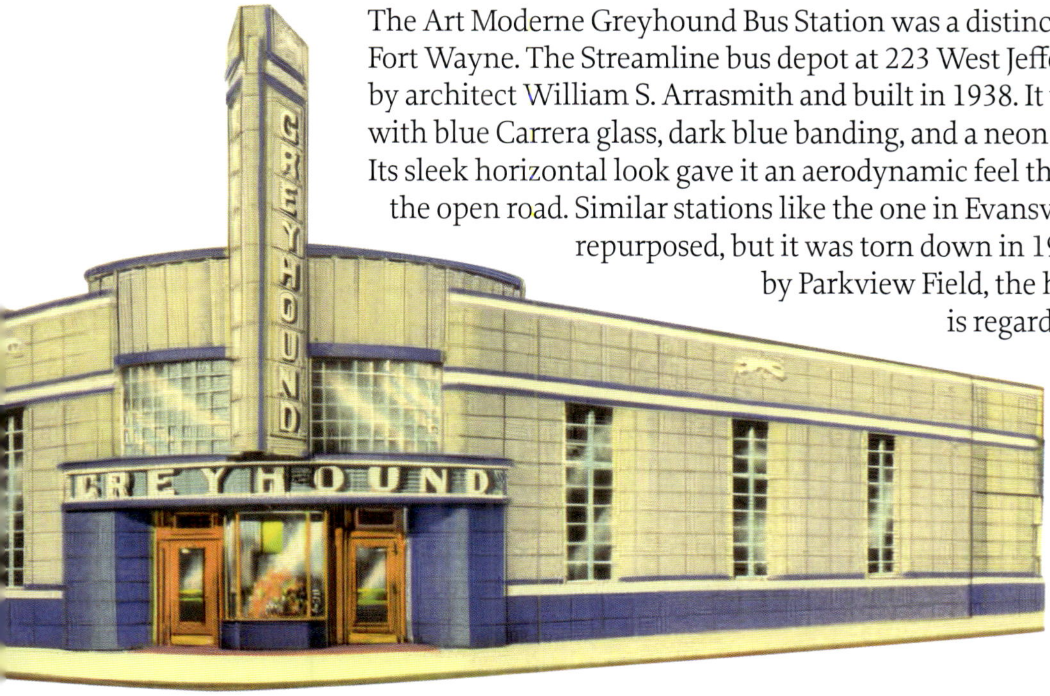

Courtesy of the Evansville Vanderburgh Public Library

Original Marion County Courthouse

The original three-story Marion County Courthouse boasted ornate Baroque architecture and a 280-foot clock tower. Isaac Hodgson designed the stately building, which was constructed in 1876 and which the *Indianapolis Daily Sentinel* described as "one of the finest, handsomest and solidest piles in the West." The entrance had a coat of arms with the Roman gods Ceres and Vulcan and the Latin phrase "Spectemur Agenda" or "Let us be judged by our actions." The courthouse at 200 East Washington also hosted city offices before City Hall was constructed in 1910. Marion County moved the courthouse to the new 373-foot-tall City-County Building in 1962, razing the old courthouse.

Courtesy of the Indianapolis-Marion County Public Library

Kokomo Gas and Fuel Tower

The Kokomo Gas and Fuel Tower was a Kokomo landmark for a half century after construction was completed in 1955. Described as "Kokomo's skyline," it stood 387 feet tall, took 2,000 gallons of paint to paint, and stored 12 million cubic feet of gas. As one of the tallest structures in Howard County, it was used by pilots at the nearby Grissom Air Force Base as a point of reference. Daredevil teens often climbed up what was locally called the Gas Tower. It fell into disuse in the early 1990s and sat vacant for a decade. The company imploded it in 2003 because it cost too much to maintain and would have cost more than $1 million to repaint. It collapsed in seconds. Pieces were salvaged, sold on plaques, and preserved at the local history museum.

Baum's Bridge

Civil War General Lew Wallace reportedly wrote the novel *Ben-Hur* in his houseboat, the *White Elephant*, while moored by Baum's Bridge over the Kankakee River. Native Americans crossed the river at a point called Pottawatomie Ford at the border of Jasper and Porter Counties. A ferry business sprang up, hauling travelers, wagons, and animals across for as little as three cents a hog. The ferry crossing was replaced with a toll bridge in 1849, but it was soon torched by an arsonist who resented having to pay a toll. The next bridge built in 1857 was destroyed by high water and ice damming. Enos Baum built the third toll bridge in 1863, which was the last toll bridge in Northwest Indiana until the Indiana Toll Road came along. The area has been known as Baum's Bridge ever since, even after Baum's wooden bridge was replaced with a steel one.

Courtesy of Steven Shook

Collier Lodge

Archaeologists have long dug up prehistoric artifacts like firepits, earthenware, and pottery at the Collier Lodge site in southern Porter County that's been occupied for more than 11,000 years. The lodge sat at a crossing point for the Kankakee River that was used by early hunter-gatherers, native tribes, fur traders, pioneers, settlers, and outdoorsmen. The Collier family built Collier Lodge in the 19th century when affluent sportsmen would visit from cities to hunt and fish. Over the decades, Collier Lodge evolved into a country inn, a general store, and a private residence. In 2022, the historic site was torn down, moved 75 feet, and rebuilt with largely new materials. Today, University of Notre Dame archaeologists comb the site for artifacts left behind, bits of history waiting to be dug out and dusted off.

Courtesy of *The Times of Northwest Indiana*

INDEX

16th Street Speedway, 67
24 Hours of Le Mans, 148
3 Floyds, 39
A&W Root Beer Barrel, 52
Aaron, Hank, 1, 71
Acapulco Joe's, 22
Anderson, 14, 17, 66, 74, 104, 110, 152, 156
Andrean High School, 168
Ann Dancing, 43
Art-Psychology Building, 166
Assumption Catholic Church, 164, 175
Atz Ice Cream, 9
Auburn, 120, 136, 149
Ball Brothers, 106, 152, 173
Ball Brothers Glass Manufacturing, 152
Ball State University, 4, 41, 76, 94, 106, 152, 173
Ball Stores, 106
Balloon races, 90
Balloon spectacle, 93
Bamboo Inn, 18
Battle of Corydon, 168
Battle of Tippecanoe, 168–169
Baum's Bridge, 181
Bear's Place, 7
Beaver Lake, 140
Bendix, 88, 157
Bendix Woods Ski Slopes, 88
Benham West, 177
Benjamin's, 8
Big Boys, 21, 35
Big Store, The, 105
Bill's Bar-B-Que, 15
Biltmore Estate, 153
Blake Gardens, 140
Bloomington, 4, 12, 14, 18, 33, 41, 48–49, 74–75, 111, 117, 122, 131, 135, 145, 153
Bon Femme, 34
Boogie Burger, 53
Breaking Away, 64, 153
Broad Ripple, 24, 36, 39, 41, 53, 61, 111, 129, 133
Bronko's Restaurant and Lounge, 9
Brown County Art Colony, 99
Brownsburg, 41
Brugge Brasserie, 41
Buggy Wheel, 21
Burger Chef, 51–52
Business Men's Association Building, The, 175
Butt Drugs, 105
Byrd, Jonathan, 25
C. G. Conn Band Instrument Factory, 155
Cadle Tabernacle, 165
Cadle, E. Howard, 165
Cafe Johnell, 34
Cafe Pizzaria, 14
Calhoun Christmas Tree Arch, 113
Camp Indiana at Indiana Dunes State Park, 119
Captain Alexander's Wharf/Moonraker, 35
Carmel, 13, 24–25, 37, 152, 162
Carriage Inn, 31
Castle Gallery, 100
Caves 'N Caverns, The, 37
Cedar Lake's Golden Resort Era, 121
Celebration Station, 3, 19
Central State Hospital, 158–159
Century Mall, 116
ChaCha, 152
Chaparral Cafe, 7
Charlie's Drive-In, 30
Chauncey Hill Mall, 115
Chez Jean, 16
Chicago, 17–18, 33, 40, 46, 49, 54, 56, 63, 68–70, 72, 77, 79, 84, 86, 90, 92, 96, 105, 107, 113, 116–119, 121, 123–125, 129–131, 133, 136, 142, 144–146, 151, 160, 176, 178
Cincinnati, 69, 71, 82, 91, 95, 106, 124–125, 145, 165
Cinema Art, 79
Cinemat, The, 75
Circle Centre Mall, 36, 45, 110, 114
Circle Park, 143
Circus Capital of the World, 88
City Methodist Church, 165
Clabber Girl Museum, 95
Clarksville Seafood, 32

Claypool Hotel, 118
College Football Hall of Fame, 95
Collier Lodge, 181
Colts, 25, 36, 65, 68, 70, 178
Country Lounge, 46
Cowboy Bob, 26, 125
Culver, 52, 121, 167
Culver Main Barrack, 167
Culver's Golden Resort Era, 121
DC's Country Junction, 85
Dean, James, 19, 73, 99, 163
Deer Creek, 82
DePauw University, 26, 145
Don Davis of Don's Guns, 126
Ducky's Family Restaurant, 15
Duesenberg, 120, 136, 149
Dunaway's Palazzo Ossigeno, 46
Dunes Arcade Hotel, 120
Eagle's Nest, 6
El Barrio, 177
El Frio, 56
Elbow Room, 42
Elkhart, vi, 15, 52, 94, 110, 136, 146, 152, 155, 177
Empire Quarry, 153
Empire State building, 153
Empress Court, 28
Enchanted Forest, 61
English Hotel and Opera House, 87
Evansville, vi, 4, 12, 17, 19, 64, 87, 89, 94, 124, 128, 146, 156, 164, 175, 179
Evansville Shipyard, 156
Everglades of the North, 137, 139
Fair Oaks Mall, 116
Fairmount High School, 163
Fairview Park, 142
Fall Creek Parkway, 38
Felt Buildings, 176
Fetla's Trading Post, 107
Fever, 68, 173
Fiddler's Hearth, 29, 39
Flakey Jake's, 27
Flanagan's Restaurant & Pub, 20
Flatiron Building, 42, 178
Fort Harrison, 169
Fort Ouiatenon, 170
Fort Sackville, 168
Fort Wayne, 2, 9, 20, 34–35, 41, 48, 50, 69–70, 94, 100, 102, 112–113, 124, 128–129, 169, 174, 179
Fort Wayne Mad Ants, 69
Fort Wayne News-Sentinel, 129
Fort Wayne Pistons, 70
Fort Wayne's 1816 Fort, 169
Franciscan Health Hammond, 160
Frank C. Ball Mansion, 173
Frank-N-Stein, 5
French and Indian War, 168, 170
French Grand Prix, 149
French Lick, 1, 55, 144, 160
Gardner's Drive-In/Char-King, 50
Garfield, 58, 163
Gary, vi, 5, 9, 53, 56, 59, 68, 70–71, 74, 80, 83, 116, 119, 123, 128, 133, 136, 149, 151, 165–166, 176
Gary American, 133
Gary Bears, 70
Gary Dawgs, 68
Gary Sheraton, 119
Gary Steelheads, 71
Gennett Records, 82
GM, 147, 156
Gnaw Bone, 4
Grand Leader/Stillman's, 112
Grand Theater, 89, 175
Grandy's, 12
Grassyfork Fisheries, 155
Graves, Michael, 1, 174
Gray Brothers Cafeteria, 15
Great Depression, 38, 56, 88, 106, 130, 146–147, 149–150
Greyhound Bus Depot, 179
Haag Drugs, 108
Haggis, 42
Hall's Original Drive-In, 48
Hammer's Food & Drink, 30
Hammond, vi, 4, 54, 58, 72, 77, 84, 96, 102–103, 116, 131, 136, 160, 162, 176
Hammond Pros, 72
Hammer, Steve, 129
Harley-Davidson, 1, 65
Harlow Hickenlooper, 127
Harrison, Benjamin, 145, 167, 169, 172
Harroun, Ray, 150
Harry's Chocolate Shop, 39

Hartford Whalers, 69
Hawthorn Restaurant, 16
Heavilon Hall, 163
Hegewisch Records, 84, 130
Herron Art Institute, 98, 101
Hilton U. Brown Theatre, 90
Hindostan, 173
Hog Boys, 65
Hole, The, 107
Holly House, 25
Honey Creme Donut Shop, 30
Hook's Drug Stores, 108
Hoosier Dome, 65
Hoosier Slide, 137, 141, 152
Horace A. Tuttle Shipwreck, 172
Host, Ghost, 82, 89, 100, 102, 125
Hot Potato, 131
Huddle Restaurants, The, 48
Hummer, 157
Hunt, Lamar, 27, 29, 167, 181
Illusions, 37
iMOCA, 100
Indiana Avenue, 15, 81, 85
Indiana Aviation Museum, 97
Indiana Dunes, 61, 89, 98, 118–120, 138, 141, 170
Indiana National Bank, 6, 179
Indiana State Sanatorium, 159
Indiana State University, 145
Indiana Theater, 78
Indiana University, vi, 7, 12, 14, 40, 56, 64, 67, 71, 75, 85, 91, 99, 101, 126, 134
Indianapolis, vi, 2–4, 6, 8, 11, 13–14, 16–18, 22–23, 25–29, 32, 36–38, 41–45, 47–48, 50–53, 55, 57, 61, 63–67, 69–71, 73, 81–82, 85, 90–91, 93–95, 98, 100–102, 106, 108–111, 114–115, 117–118, 124–133, 136, 138, 142–143, 145, 147–150, 158–159, 161, 165, 171–172, 177–180
Indianapolis 500, 25, 64, 66, 90, 93, 110, 148–150
Indianapolis Clowns, 67, 71
Indianapolis Leader, 132
Indianapolis News, 132
Indianapolis Racers, 69
Indianapolis Tennis Center, 67
Indianapolis Times, 4, 130
Interurban Elkhart County, 146
Irish Lion, 40
Iron Skillet, 28
Irvine, Robert, 15, 29
Janie, 126
Jazz at the Station, 12
Jim Dandy, 21, 49
John Dillinger Museum, 96
Jonathan Byrd's, 25
Jones, Scott, 49, 71, 152, 176
Jong Mea, 10
Jungle Park Speedway, 66
Key West Shrimp House, 14
Kilroy's, 39
King Cole, 8
King, Martin Luther, 8, 25, 30, 32, 39, 50, 52, 54, 71, 73, 85, 104, 142, 165, 177
King's Grocery, 104
Kirkwood Avenue, 14, 18, 40, 75
Knobby's Restaurant, 17
Kokomo, 1, 15, 110, 134, 143, 147, 152, 174, 180
Kokomo Gas and Fuel Tower, 180
Kokomo Perspective, 134
L. S. Ayres and Company, 109
L. Strauss and Co., 110
La Porte Herald-Argus, 134
La Porte Theatre, 92
La Tour, 6
Lake Maxinkuckee, 121, 167
Lake Michigan, 1, 4–5, 70, 91, 96, 118–119, 121–122, 133, 137–138, 141, 151, 170–172
Lasers on the Dunes, 89
Laughing Planet, 18
Le Petit Fort, 170
Lido Supper Club, The, 29
Limberlost Swamp, 136, 139
Lincoln Museum, The, 94
Little Nashville Opry, 83
Littleville, 99
Lotus Garden, 4
Louisville, 16, 31, 33, 63, 124, 145–146, 174
Louisville and Nashville Union Depot, 146
Lowenstine's Department Store, 112
Lure, The, 53
Mac's Hideaway, 33
MacNiven's, 42
Macri's Italian Village, 13
Maennerchor Club, 91
Mandarin Inn, 4
Marion International Motorcycle Race, 65

Market Square Arena, 64, 69
Marmon, 147, 150
Marsh Supermarkets, 106
Mascot Hall of Fame, 96
Maumee River, 169
Meis Department Store, 110
Melody Inn, 39
Merchants National Bank, 178
Merrill's Hi-Decker, 11
Mesker Park Zoo Monkey House, 87
Middletown, 152
Midwest Beat Magazine, 84, 131
Milano Inn, 26
Miller Beach, 5
Mineral water, 55, 161
Mineral Water Sanitariums, 160
Minnetrista, 124, 152, 173
Mishawaka, 22, 41, 79, 146–147, 157, 161
Mnomen, 141
Moderne Sweet Shop, The, 25
Monon Railroad, 117, 121, 145
Monon Restaurant, 26
Mr. Happy Burger, 32
Mudbugs, 3, 24
Muncie, 10, 41, 52, 76–77, 104–106, 124, 141, 152, 173
Nabors, Jim, 26
National Register of Historic Places, 66, 79, 158
New Albany, 30, 33, 154, 173
New Albany Glass Works, 154
New Albany Shipyards, 154
New Auburn Hotel, 120
Nick's English Hut, 39, 49
Nickel Plate Bar and Grill, 43
Nicky Blaine's, 8
Night Rock News, 130
Noblesville, 21, 41, 69, 82
Northwoods, 38
Nuvo Print Edition, 129
Old Ben, 143, 174
Old Point Tavern, 43
Old Style Inn, 45
Original Marion County Courthouse, 180
Oscar C. McCulloch School No. 5, 164
Owen J. Bush Stadium, 67
Pacers, 64, 66, 68–69
Palace Theater, The, 74
Palomino, 45
Parrott-Taggart Crackers, 57
Patio, The, 11, 41
Peerless Potato Chips, 55
Pembroke Arcade, 115
Penguin Point, 21, 32
Peppy Grill, 50
Petty, Tom, 67, 80
Philadelphia, The, 23, 94, 107
Phoenix Theatre, 92
Pie Pan, 19
Pines, The, 31, 91
Pines Peak, 88, 91
Pit of Despair, 107
Plainfield, 16, 47
Plan 9 Film Emporium, 74
Pluto Water, 56
Poe's Cafeteria, 35
Pogue's Run, 142
Polk's Best Jersey Milk, 57
Pork tenderloin sandwich, 2
Pogue's Run, 142
Premier Theater, The, 79
Puck, Wolfgang, 1, 6
Purdue University, vi, 67, 101, 115, 123, 163
Q.L.'s Bar-B-Que, 10
Rangel, Joe, 22
Red Gold, 2, 54
Red Lantern Inn, 30, 118
Red Light District, 90
Restaurant Impossible, 15
Richmond, 36, 52, 82
Riley Park Drive-In, 49
Riverside, 61
Rivoli Theatre, 77
Robinson, Glen "Big Dog", 79, 166
Rocky's Sub Pub, 31
Rodini's, 5
Rolls-Royce, 149
Roosevelt High School, 166
Ropkey Armor Museum, 97
Rose Island, 63
Roselyn Bakery, 55
Ruschman Art Gallery, 101

RV, 1, 94, 136, 155
Ryder, The, 135
Sammy Terry, 125
Santorini's, 23
Sauzer's Kiddieland, 62
Scotty's Brewhouse, 2, 41
Seaman, William, 165
Sedley Bridge, 175
Shakey's Pizza Parlor, 13
Shepherd, Jean, 20, 40, 77, 102, 116, 124
Sir Beef, 17
Siskel, Gene, 167
Ski-Hi Drive-In, 76
Slippery Noodle Inn, 2, 39, 43
Smithsonian, 106
Snooty Fox, 29
Snyderman House, 174
Soldiers and Sailors Monument, 143, 172
Sousa, John Philip, 93, 172
South Bend, 5, 13, 22–23, 25–27, 29, 35, 52, 94–95, 107, 111, 123–124, 128, 140, 144, 148, 153, 157
Spanish Castle, 176
St. Elmo's Steak House, 2, 44, 45
St. Francis Beech Grove, 160
St. Joseph River, 35, 141, 153
St. Mary's River, 169
Star Plaza, 19, 81, 131
State Line Slaughterhouse, 160
Steak 'N Shake, 2, 51
Steel mill, 68, 165, 176
Steinbrenner, George, 167
Stratton-Porter, Gene, 139
Strongbow Inn, 6
Studebaker, 136, 148
Stutz, Harry, 136, 148
Sumner, Dick, 11
Sunset Terrace, 85
Swamp Act, 139
Svengoolie, 125
Sycamore Stump, 143
Taggart Baking Company, 57
Tee Pee Restaurants, 38
Terre Haute, 40, 48, 66, 78, 90, 93, 95, 110, 117, 124, 145, 152, 169
Terre Haute Brewing Company, 40
Terre Haute Grand Opera House, 93
Terre Haute House, 117
Terre Haute Union Station, 145
Tin Star, 36
Tivoli Theatre, The, 76
Tomlinson Hall, 172
Town Theatre, 77
Trolley, 63, 142, 146
Union Jack Pub, 39
Valentino, Rudoph, 172
Valparaiso, 6, 13, 20, 34, 36, 46, 54, 79, 88, 91, 97, 107, 112, 166, 175
Vee-Jay Records, 83
Village Pantry, 7, 18, 106
Village Sampler, 133
Von Lee, 75
Wabash College, 24, 145
Wabash River, 168–170
Waffle House, 49, 62
White House, The, 20, 22
Wayne, Mad Anthony, 69, 169
West Baden Springs, 55, 117, 160
West Race, 153
White House Restaurant, 22
White River, 10, 61, 67, 133, 156, 164, 173
WIBC, 11
Wigwam, 66
William H. Block Co., 111
Wimpy, 33, 48
Wolf & Dessauer, 102, 113
Wonderland Amusement Park, 61, 63
Wooden Keg, 27
Woodmar Records, 84
World War I, 56, 91, 95, 97, 146
World War II, 13, 17, 35, 38, 67, 82, 97, 99, 108, 134, 146, 148–149, 156, 166, 174
WSBT, 155
Wyman's Department Store, 111
Y & W Drive-In in Merrillville, 78
Yats, 24
Zipper Building, 178